Lessons from Danny

Also By Jenny Hagemeyer

"Touch Me Guide to Healing"
(companion study book to "Touch Me")
"Touch Me"

Available at:
Local Bookstores
Amazon.com
Barnes and Noble
iUniverse.com

Lessons from Danny

Jenny Hagemeyer

iUniverse LLC
Bloomington

LESSONS FROM DANNY

Scripture quotations marked AMP are taken from the AMPLIFIED BIBLE, Old Testament copyright @ 1965 by the Zondervan Corporation. The Amplified New Testament copyright 1958, 1987 by the Lockman Foundation. Used by permission.

Scripture quotations marked NIV are taken from the NEW INTERNATIONAL VERSION. Copyright @ 1973, 1978, 1984 by International Bible Society, Used by permission of Zondervan Publishing House. All rights reserved.

Scripture quotations taken from The Message copyright @ 1993, 1994, 1995, 1996, 2000, 2001, 2002 used by permission of Nav Press Publishing Group.

iUniverse books may be ordered through booksellers or by contacting:

iUniverse LLC
1663 Liberty Drive
Bloomington, IN 47403
www.iuniverse.com
1-800-Authors (1-800-288-4677)

ISBN: 978-1-4917-1685-4 (sc)
ISBN: 978-1-4917-1686-1 (e)

Printed in the United States of America.

iUniverse rev. date: 01/15/2014

Contents

Acknowledgments

Father . . . we exalt you as our Creator, Master, Lord and Holy God! Your redemptive love is amazing. You gave your only unique Son to die on the cross to save us from our sin. We believe in Jesus and the redeeming work of the cross therefore, we will not perish but have everlasting life with you. Thank you for your Son, Jesus who became our sacrifice and paid the penalty for our sin. (John 3:16)

Jesus . . . you lived a perfect life that gave us a path to follow after your heart. You chose to suffer a cruel death on the cross when you could have called ten thousand angels to rescue you. Yet, in obedience to our Father you bore the abandonment that should have been ours. You were utterly alone so that we may never be alone. You conquered sin and death and all the powers of hell and took back the keys that unlocked the door to the Kingdom of God so we could be one with our Father. You gave us your last supper that brought in the new covenant of grace so we would no longer fail at trying to change ourselves by the old covenant law. Your communion with bread represents your body that was broken for us. The cup of wine represents your blood that was poured out on the cross for us. We now have an intimate personal relationship with you and receive healing spiritually, emotionally, mentally, relationally and physically. After your resurrection, you told your disciples that you must join your Father in heaven so the Holy Spirit (comforter) would come.

Holy Spirit . . . As the disciples gathered in the upper room to receive Your power and to be filled with the Holy Spirit, You brought conviction and led them into all truth. As you continue to be God's voice within us, you speak inspiration, wisdom, encouragement, revelation and direction to us from our Father God.

> **"But when he, the Spirit of truth, comes, he will guide you into all the truth. He will not speak on his own; he will speak only what he hears, and he will tell you what is yet to come. He will glorify me because it is from me that he will receive what he will make known to you."(John 16:13-14 NIV)**

Thank you, Father, Jesus and Holy Spirit for giving me the honor of being used as your vessel to bring healing and inspiration to your children. You gave me the dream of saving Danny which led me to know that his life was in the palm of your hands. Little did I know that I would write a third book under the inspiration of the Holy Spirit!

Thank you, Fred, my husband for not giving up on pursuing your desire for a dog even when I didn't want another one. What a blessing Danny is to both of us!

Thank you, Mom, for taking care of Danny when we aren't able to take him with us. Thank you for also sharing every book that I have written with your friends and encouraging me to finish this book.

Thank you, Gary and Joan for your persistence in calling us and being the vessels that God used to direct us to have a second opinion on Danny.

Thank you Centre Animal Hospital for showing your love and caring hearts to us and our little Danny! We thank God for leading us to you that gave Danny a longer life with us!

Thank you, Regina for our friendship and the many hours you spent looking over each page for editing my third book. Thank you for all of your encouragement and enthusiasm every time I am working on another book!

Thank you, Andrew for the hours you spent working on the graphics design for my book cover.

Thank you, all of my sisters in the Promise Land Ministries team and the women who attend the "Touch Me" studies weekly for your love and encouragement in publishing this book.

I am so blessed to have all of you in my life!

Introduction

Most of us have heard the saying, "Boy! He has a dog's life!" Well, that is what we say when we see someone who has an easy life. But . . . did you ever think of what your pet would say about their life? When you are feeling discouraged, do they pick this up too? When you cry does your pet feel the sadness in your heart and kiss your tears? What about when they want to play and you ignore them since you are too busy. When your pet greets you at the door, do you make them feel as important as you are to them?

I was outside walking Danny, our little mixed Shih Tzu the other day. Another dog came running out of the neighbor's driveway after Danny. Suddenly, I heard his master calling him to come back, however, his dog kept his focus on Danny and kept moving towards him. His master came outside to stop him from coming after Danny. Suddenly the dog stopped and began to walk close to his master. My neighbor told me that his dog wouldn't hurt our dog; he is just being friendly and is a good dog. He said people say that dogs pick up our traits. He told me that his dog tends to be stubborn just like him. We laughed about this but I thought about how Danny reacts when I am sad. He jumps on my lap and kisses my tears. When either one of us is sick, he lies by our side as he senses something is wrong with us. When we rescued Danny from the SPCA, immediately we saw how loving and sweet he was. The girls in the Promise Land Ministries team told us that he fit right in with the ministry!

Many of us place God in a neat tidy box and think He will only do certain things for us. After all, this is only a dog and not a human being. One morning I was in my vehicle driving to a class to teach the "Touch Me" study that I had written under the inspiration of the Holy Spirit! I had written Danny's testimony from my perspective but now I was hearing in my spirit an altogether different version. I realized God was showing me to write Danny's testimony as though Danny would relay it if he could speak. After the class was over, I was excited to see what the Holy Spirit had written on my heart. I sat down at my computer and said, "Lord, if this is how you want to write this, please give me your wisdom and inspiration. The Holy Spirit inspired me to write "Lessons from Danny" as though Danny was speaking. As I wrote this, the Holy Spirit led me to write lessons that I had learned from Danny that have impacted my life!

My prayer is that as you read "Lessons from Danny" this will inspire you to hunger and thirst for more of God. I encourage you to take Him out of the box. Allow God to do far above what you could ever think or imagine and infinitely beyond your highest prayers, desires, thoughts, hopes or dreams!

> **"Now to Him Who, by (in consequence of) the (action of His) power that is at work within us, is able to (carry out His purpose and) do superabundantly, far over *and* above all that we (dare) ask or think (infinitely beyond our highest prayers, desires, thoughts, hopes, or dreams) To Him be glory in the church and in Christ Jesus throughout all generations forever and ever." Amen (so be it). (Ephesians 3:20-21 AMP)**

God loves you,

Jenny

The Beginning

I hope you'll excuse how I look today . . . . I'm having a bad hair day! I was scheduled to get a haircut but it didn't work out with my groomer this week. I really try not to get upset when my plans don't work out but . . . I'm sorry to say that sometimes my flesh takes over my spirit. Hey! Anybody out there have that problem too? **Isaiah 43:2 says, "When you pass through the water, I will be with you, and through the rivers, they will not overwhelm you. When you walk through the fire you will not be burned or scorched, nor will the flame kindle upon you." (AMP)** Well, sometimes life comes at us fast and throws us a curve that we are not expecting! God doesn't always take us out of our situations in this life but His promise is to take us through them. However, it's our choice to **Hold onto His hand** or let go and try to make it on our own! My name is Danny and I am a little mixed Shih Tzu. Mommy asked me to give you my testimony so . . . here goes! My mommy calls me her little brown eyed blonde and sometimes her angel from heaven since she believes that I was brought to her and Daddy by God. However, my daddy calls me a two time loser! Now, before you get really upset with my dad there is a reason he calls me this.

I was just a puppy when I suddenly was placed into an SPCA! I guess I was too little to remember why? But I do remember not being there very long when a couple came to rescue me. I don't remember them very well but I know they must have taught me a lot since I have very good manners and I am a very sweet and loving little guy. What I don't understand is why they only had me for one and one half years and took me back to the SPCA. Now do you see why Daddy calls me a two time loser?

I couldn't believe that I was all bound up in a cage again. Three days passed when suddenly a couple showed up that really had their attention on me. I liked the man right away and thought "He will make a good Daddy!" When he petted me I thought "I like this one, Lord!" The lady that was with him didn't have the excitement that I saw in this man in petting me. But I thought to myself, "She can't help not to love me. I'll give her lots of kisses and that will melt her heart!"

Listening to everyone talk, I found out their names were Fred and Jenny. The next thing I knew I was being whisked out of the SPCA and going bye byes with this couple. I took a whiff of the fresh air and thought "AAAH! My life is looking up!" Jenny placed me on her lap and suddenly began to cry. I looked up at her and kissed her. Later I found out that Fred and Jenny had a Lhasa Apsa that had been put to sleep ten years ago and Jenny didn't want to get attached to another dog. God showed Jenny why she was crying with me. He told her that she never took the time to grieve over Benji since she felt to buck up since he was a dog and not a person. God had showed her that is why she didn't want a dog. God was healing her through me. Imagine that! Fred and Jenny showed me my new house. Boy! I liked them right away. They called themselves Mommy and Daddy! Yay! I had a new Mommy and Daddy that really liked me. Mommy sat me down one day and told me how they found me. She told me that she didn't want a dog but Daddy kept trying to show her all different ones hoping to change her mind.

Finally, one night Mommy was talking to God about it. She heard Him say, "You didn't ask me!" She said, "I didn't know that I was supposed to!" Now you need to understand that Mommy talks to God out loud and Mommy says God talks in our insides. I think she calls it your spirit. You see . . . Mommy and God talk to each other every day and she is very gut honest with Him! Well, when she asked "Okay, God what do you want me to do?" He told her to let Fred go and He would lead him to the dog. Well, Daddy was really happy when Mommy told him what God said. So that's why Mommy calls me her little angel from heaven!

The Diagnosis

I have been living with Mommy and Daddy for almost five years. We don't know when to celebrate my birthday but the veterinarian said I was about two or three years old when they got me. Last year something began to happen in my eyes. I would rub them since I wasn't able to see very clearly. The veterinarian told us that I had glaucoma in one eye and a cataract on the other eye. Mommy asked God what was going on with me. That night God said, "Take authority over the curse of blindness in Danny!" Mommy didn't understand why God said that but she obeyed! I've really learned that you don't always have to understand everything but when God says to do something . . . Do It!

Later on Mommy found out that Shih Tzu's can have a problem with their eyes. Mommy knew that it was a generational curse! About one month later Mommy had this dream. Now you need to understand that Mommy doesn't believe that all dreams are from God but she knew this one was. I was out in very deep water and was about to drown. Mommy swam out to rescue me. She was able to grab hold of me just in time and realized that her body was being held above the water. She turned around and saw a ship that was as big as a cruise ship not only heading in our direction but coming straight for us. Mommy had to make a choice to let me go and save herself or stay and hold onto me. She put her head down and held me in her arms. Suddenly the ship went over us without touching us or harming us in any way. Mommy began to pray every day over my eyes and for my protection.

February ninth, seven months after the dream, I suddenly got very ill so Daddy took me to the veterinarian. The news hit us like a ton of bricks and made Mommy and Daddy cry over me. The veterinarian said I had a mass on my stomach the size of a softball and also had anemia. He told them that I had less than one week to live. He suggested that it would probably be better to put me to sleep. You see my red blood cell count was down so low that there was only a five per cent chance of surviving the surgery! How could this be? After all, God brought my mommy and daddy to me.

Mommy remembered the dream and told Daddy so he went down to the veterinarian's office and picked me up since I was there for x-rays! I don't mind telling you that when I heard the news, I was really scared that I wouldn't see my mommy and daddy ever again but suddenly Daddy showed up and brought me home. I wanted to kiss Daddy but just didn't have the strength. Mommy and Daddy took me into their arms and gave me to Jesus and asked for His wisdom. They told Him that they were giving Him the opportunity to show Himself strong in my body. In the evening I ate a little liver since that has iron in it . . . . but I just didn't feel up to eating very much. Actually, I didn't feel very good and just felt to lie around. Is anybody out there feeling sick like I was? Did you get a bad report from the doctor? Let us know and we'll pray for you!

Days before surgery!

The next day was Saturday. This is one of my favorite days since I get to hang out with both Mommy and Daddy. Sometimes Mommy makes a cooked breakfast and I get some samples. Well, Mommy was drinking her usual cup of coffee as she walked into the living room and sat down. Daddy was watching his usual news programs. Mommy couldn't believe her eyes. On the television during a commercial break, she saw in big letters . . . . BELIEVE! Then she began to sing a song! I still wasn't feeling too good but I loved to listen to Mommy sing. Well, I heard her sing, "I believe in you, My Lord! I believe in you, My King! I believe in you, My Lord! You are My Everything!" I could see that Mommy was receiving encouragement from the Lord since she always feels better when she is singing praises to Him!

Again Mommy and Daddy prayed and called all of my organs and red blood cells into alignment. I didn't understand this but I trusted that Daddy and Mommy knew what to say! The phone rang and it was my Uncle Gary. He thought I should have a second opinion with his veterinarian. Mommy and Daddy said they would pray and ask the Lord what He wanted them to do. That evening Mommy and Daddy went away without me. I wasn't happy about staying by myself but I did start to feel a little better and greeted them at the door with my toy when they came home. I could see Mommy and Daddy's eyes light up. That made me happy to see them happy!

The next day was church day. I know that Mommy and Daddy's pastor won't let me go to church even if I promise to be good. Therefore, I always have to be alone and wear a diaper in case I have an accident. To tell you the truth, this is quite embarrassing but Mommy persists even when I try to hide from her or make it very difficult for her. Well, I heard Mommy tell Daddy about another dream she had that night. As far as I could make out she said there was a woman who was quite ill. Mommy asked her what her diagnosis was. I'm not sure what that word means. But the woman told her what disease she had and that the doctor told her the progression of the disease would worsen. Mommy's spirit immediately rose up. She said, "No . . . we aren't accepting this. God gave you your parts and satan can't steal them". Well, Mommy's spirit was so strong that she talked like that over me. She told satan every part of my body that he couldn't have and believe you me she meant it!

In the afternoon Mommy read a scripture to me. I love when Mommy reads to me. It makes me feel better. She read from Lamentations . . . that book sounds like a lot of sadness to me. The author Jeremiah is known as the weeping Prophet. I can't understand why he was always crying. Well, **Lamentations 3:37-38 in the NIV says, "Who can speak and have it happen if the Lord has not decreed it? Is it not from the mouth of the Most High that both calamities and good things come?"**

I'm not sure what NIV stands for but I think it's a New Intravenous Injection into someone's vein. Well, this Word sure did give Mommy a shot in the arm! Mommy said, "Decreed means the will or purpose of God and declare means to state emphatically or announce". Mommy knew that if God didn't decree for me to live longer, I wouldn't! Mommy could announce it all she wanted but God had the final say! So the question was . . . Did God decree healing for me? Mommy and Daddy had to surrender their will for my healing and accept God's will and purpose in all of these events leading up to now!

Again, my Uncle Gary called and asked Mommy and Daddy what they decided. They were still praying and waiting on God.

In the evening Mommy was watching television. A preview of a program showed someone who had been murdered and lying in a pool of blood. A detective was observing this incident and made this comment, "The truth is in the blood!" Immediately, the Holy Spirit spoke to Mommy. He said, "The truth is in the blood of Jesus!" I was lying in front of the mantel feeling very tired. Mommy laid hands on me and pleaded the blood of Jesus over every area of my body. I heard her talk to Jesus about the Israelites and how they put the blood over the door post so the death angel would pass by. Mommy said the death angel would pass over me and I would live. Now before some of you start getting bent out of shape on pleading the blood of Jesus over a dog, Mommy asked the Lord if she was really hearing from Him. God asked her a question in her insides. He said "You plead the blood of Jesus over your property, don't you? Isn't Danny your property too? One day Mommy heard a preacher talk about a scripture that includes blessings on pets too.

> Deuteronomy 28:1-4 says, "If you will listen diligently to the voice of the Lord your God, being watchful to do all His commandments which I command you this day, the Lord your God will set you high above all the nations of the earth. And all these blessings shall come upon you and overtake you if you heed the voice of the Lord your God. Blessed shall you be in the city and blessed shall you be in the field. Blessed shall be the fruit of your body and the fruit of your ground and the fruit of your beasts, the increase of your cattle and the young of your flock." (AMP)

Mommy knew that she was hearing from the Holy Spirit. Well, I didn't understand what she meant by everything she said but I'm sure glad she prayed it!

Monday morning my Uncle Gary called again. I watched Mommy and Daddy kind of perk up to this now. Maybe these calls are from God through my uncle. After all, this is three times. Mommy says when something happens three times God is trying to get your attention! Later that day Mommy got a call from one of the precious ladies in their ministry team. Did I tell you how much I love to see the ladies come to our house? I sit up on the couch watching and greet each one with my toys as they come in the door! Well, an evangelist was in town all week with a healing service and this precious lady was inviting my mommy to come. Mommy knew the only night she had to go was that night. Mommy and Daddy were finishing their supper when the phone rang again. This time . . . . I heard some more bad news. My grandpa was sick in his kidneys and only had four percent operation of them. Mommy said she was going to stand proxy for Grandpa and me at the service that night. Mommy said she never heard of anyone standing proxy for a dog but she thought . . . what could it hurt? I didn't know what she was going to stand on but I knew what Mommy said she would do.

Mommy came home and said the evangelist agreed with her for healing so again she laid hands on me and prayed. Then I heard her tell Daddy that a lady came to her before the service and gave her testimony of healing on her dad's dog and horse. Mommy seemed so encouraged! I knew God must be really working! Daddy told her that he talked with the veterinarian that Uncle Gary had told her about. She said that I may have a ruptured spleen. Whoa! I sure hoped not! That sounded really serious. Believe me, I didn't feel up to being prodded and poked at! Well, Daddy made an appointment on . . . of all days . . . . Valentine's Day!

It's Time for Surgery . . .
Valentine's Day!

Daddy bought a card for me to give Mommy and she cried. It said, "I wish we could give you all the flowers in the world . . . but instead, we'll give you all the love in our heart (and all our hugs and kisses too!)" Daddy had me sign it by placing my paws into something and then on the card! But you should have seen Daddy's card to Mommy. It was 20 times bigger than mine and she put it on a stand in our living room! She put mine on the stand too! Guess Mommy was really happy to have cards from both of her guys!

On the way to the veterinarian, Mommy saw an eagle up in the sky. She said that is how God wants us to be . . . . flying above our circumstances in this life. Of course, I didn't really know where we were going. I just thought I was going bye byes! A couple of miles further up the road Mommy saw a sign that said, "God Speed!" Again she pointed that out too! Mommy hadn't had time for devotions with God that morning so she brought her Bible with her. She opened it up to **Romans 8:28 that says, "We are assured *and* know that (God being a partner in their labor) all things work together *and* are (fitting into a plan) for good to *and* for those who love God and are called according to (His) design and purpose." (AMP)** Mommy said that she had to view my sickness as an opportunity for God to show Himself strong in our life! Whoa! That's not really easy to do is it? Especially, when you are smack dab in the middle of a crisis! But we all knew that God was showing us His presence in the eagle, sign, and His Word! Somehow God was going to bring blessings out of all these disappointments and difficulties that we were experiencing! After all, God was our partner in all this labor!

So . . . let me tell you about my veterinarians. Daddy and Mommy were praying for wisdom and God sent us to really smart doctors. What a blessing they were! They were so nice and gentle with me. I liked them right away and so did Daddy and Mommy.

After running tests, they explained that I had a ruptured spleen. However, my red blood cell count was elevated enough to operate that day. Wow! Believe me, it wasn't the liver since I wouldn't eat that much on Friday evening. So . . . what was it? I believe it was God that touched my red blood cells through many people praying. My daddy and mommy believe this too. Now instead of five percent chance of recovering from surgery I was given a sixty percent chance. But if the mass was on my liver my life would have been over. Daddy and Mommy knew that God could heal me without an operation however, God also heals with surgery. Daddy felt to go for it but Mommy was still wavering until she heard God say, "Trust Me!" She felt God's peace to trust Him with my life and for their finances so she decided to say yes to the surgery!

So . . . Daddy and Mommy released me from their hands and placed me completely into God's hands! I couldn't see Jesus but I felt His hands wrap around my body to protect me from any harm. Mommy says that God enfolds His children under His everlasting arms to protect them from the enemy. If you need Jesus to protect you, He is there waiting to enfold His arms around you and protect your heart and mind from the enemy of your soul. Just do like Mommy and Daddy did. Call on His name and He'll come running to your rescue.

After the Surgery

The next thing I remembered was the surgeon standing over me as I was coming out of the anesthesia. My thought was "I've had enough of this. I'm out of here!" So I began to walk off the table but she took hold of me and laid me down. When I was more awake I was bundled up and put in a vehicle. I thought "Oh! No! Where are they taking me?" Maybe they will bring me to my house. But when we entered the building the smell was very familiar and I knew that it wasn't my home. I wanted to shout, "Let me out of here"! But I was still very weak and couldn't make a lot of noise so I remained quiet. I realized that I just had to accept what was happening to me even when I didn't like it! In the Bible **I Timothy 6:6 says, "Godliness with contentment is great gain!"** **(NIV)** Well, to tell you the truth I didn't feel very godly about all of this nor did I like what I felt in my belly! I felt funny inside like something was missing in me but didn't know what it was. Later I found out that they took my spleen. Hey, guys did you know that dogs can live without a spleen? Sorry! I don't know about cats or humans! During the night people kept checking up on me. I wasn't very happy that I was in a cage again but I was too weak to protest! The next morning I got awake and would you believe another person put me in a vehicle. I thought maybe this time they are taking me home! But I realized this is where I was before and again those familiar smells were in my nostrils! "Please God! I want to go home!" They gave me something to eat but come on let's get real! How do you feel after surgery? Do you feel like eating? Again I was placed into a cage. This time I made up my mind that I was sitting in the front and was not going to sit back in that cage. Maybe if I kept looking at them with my big sad brown eyes they would take pity on me and let me out! Well, finally after many hours too numerous to mention I was out!

The doctor picked me up and placed me in her arms and carried me into a room. I thought now what are they going to do to me. Doesn't this ever end? She opened the door and suddenly I saw my daddy and mommy. I still wasn't myself so I didn't greet them even though I really wanted too! My daddy seemed so disappointed that I didn't get excited over him like I usually do. Mommy held me on her lap and hugged me. I didn't respond very well since I was so frail and weak. I found out later that the surgery was supposed to take forty minutes to an hour but ended up taking three and one half hours. No wonder I was so tired! I was under anesthesia for a long time but the good news is that I didn't need any blood transfusions! Mommy says that Jesus gave us a blood transfusion when He was crucified on the cross. In order to start the flow of God's love to our cold hearts, He became the donor who gave His precious blood for all of His creation! Wow! Think of that! When you truly grasp God's love for you, your life will never be the same. By the way, I lost two pounds since that's how heavy the mass was. Well, nobody can call me fatty anymore! And since I'm still alive I'm sure you guessed there was no spot on my liver. Hooray! God had declared my life to continue on!

In the evening Daddy and Mommy had to force feed me since I was just too tired to eat or drink. All I wanted to do was sleep with my daddy and mommy on their bed. Just as I started to doze off the phone rang! Boy! That phone rings a lot! I heard Mommy talking to someone about Grandma and she sounded very upset. I thought "Oh! No! What's wrong with my grandma? You see . . . . I really like my grandma since she keeps me when Daddy and Mommy go away sometimes. She lives in a cottage in a retirement village and I get to see all her friends. I know that Grandma's friends really like me since they always "ooh" and "aaah" over me! And Grandma cooks chicken just for me. You know how Grandma's can really spoil you, right? Well, Mommy said that Grandma was really sick and was being rushed to the hospital in an ambulance. You need to know that we don't live a hop, skip and a jump from Grandma's house. She lives two hours away from us. When we go to visit her I can hardly wait for the two hours to be up, but suddenly we are on this street that I always recognize. Mommy had to wait for the results from the nurse in the emergency room. Finally at midnight she found out that Grandma had the stomach flu that had been going around. Mommy says it's not fun to wait on God since we live in a microwave society. I guess she means that we want everything really quick and sometimes it seems like God is really slow! Does anyone else feel that way?

Day Two

Well, it had been two days after the surgery and Mommy and Daddy still had to force feed me in the morning. Mommy always has oatmeal and peanut butter for breakfast. She knows that is one of my favorite foods so that's what she was giving me. Mommy says that I am such a good little guy when I let her open my mouth. I never growl or show my teeth. I wouldn't think of it! After all, I know a soft answer turns away wrath. Now I will admit that if some of you dogs get aggressive with me I might let you know that enough is enough. There is a little guy named Alfie next door. He loves to sit at the window and watch for me. As soon as he sees me he begins to let his mommy or daddy know that I am outside and he wants to play with me. He comes running when he sees me. I suppose I should get excited over him too but I just don't have it in me for dogs! They just don't excite me like people do! Therefore, I tend to come off being very snobbish with Alfie. Mommy says that isn't very nice. She says that Alfie really likes me but . . . I just don't have the same feelings for him.

I was still feeling so tired and listless. I heard Mommy say that my red blood cell count needed to improve. Mommy and Daddy knew they could only do so much to help me. It was a matter of trusting that God had brought me this far and wouldn't let go! Did you ever see a bulldog holding onto a bone? Well, that's the kind of faith in God they had to have!

I could see that Daddy was really getting concerned about me but had to leave for work. Before he left he brought down something that really upset me. Of all things, it was a cage! They knew I hated those things. Actually I am ashamed to say that I turn into a different dog when I am in a cage. I guess my flesh takes over and I freak out! The veterinarian said I wasn't allowed to jump up on furniture for ten to fourteen days because my stitches could come loose. Mommy had work to do so she thought she would try placing me into that cage. I cried my little heart out so Mommy took pity on me and left me out. She didn't want to see me crying. So she put me on a chain that I could walk into the living room, kitchen and dining room. That wasn't so bad! It was a lot better than being caged up like an animal! Mommy decided to cook more liver when suddenly I got an urge to walk out and smell what she was cooking. Actually, it smelled really good so I told Mommy the best way I knew how that I wanted to eat some of it. She was so excited that she called Daddy to let him know that I ate on my own and drank water too!

This was good news but we still didn't get good news on Grandma. She was still very sick but there was nothing that Mommy could do. I know she felt so helpless. Well, isn't that how we all feel when we don't have control of a situation?

Day Three

Now we were at day three after the surgery. It was so great to feel good again! Actually, I grabbed some of my toys and told Mommy that I wanted to play by giving her lots of kisses. Now since my energy was back it was going to be harder to keep me off the furniture, but Daddy came up with an idea. He repositioned the sofa cushions. It wasn't very inviting and I actually felt a little sad since I couldn't jump up on the top of the sofa and watch for my daddy to come home. I can't even tell you how much I love my daddy! I get so excited when I hear the engine of his car. I run to my mommy and say, "Daddy's home!" Then I go over to my toy box and pull out a toy to greet my daddy. I know when I have that toy in my mouth he will begin to chase me. I love when my daddy chases me. Sometimes I hide under the table so no one sees me. Tee Hee! It makes me laugh inside. Then I see Mommy looking at me and I give her a look as if to say, "Shhh . . . don't tell Daddy where I'm hiding!" Of course, Mommy won't since she loves to watch both of us playing!

Mommy said that one day God showed her He was playing hide 'n seek with her. He told her that sometimes He hides and wants her to come after Him. Then other days God sees Mommy hiding inside herself and He comes after her! I think that means that she holds all those emotions inside her heart and doesn't tell God about it. Of course, He already knows everything in her heart so she can't hide from Him! Mommy says she loves her relationship with God. She speaks and He listens. Then Mommy waits to hear God speak and then she listens! Mommy says prayer begins with talking to God but ends with listening to His voice. That's a great relationship! Don't you think?

Well, Friday was really a great day so I found myself looking forward to being even better the next day! Will I have any setbacks?

Day Four

Oh! My! I didn't feel so good. I should have been really excited since my sister and her children were coming from out of town. I knew that I would get a lot of attention but for some reason or another I just didn't feel up to company that day! Daddy had been taking me outside to poopie but I just couldn't seem too! I just didn't know what was wrong with me. Did you ever feel that way? Some days you feel so good and other days you are just constipated. Well, in your emotions of course! Now is not the time to give up on praying.

I didn't want to go back to the veterinarians so I was trying to think positive the way Mommy says to be. Daddy and Mommy prayed for me again and asked God for His wisdom on what to do. Afterwards, we found out that Grandma was being released from the hospital. However, now she had to go into a Health Care facility. It seemed that she was weak in her legs and she needed physical therapy. Mommy says therapy is a treatment that was meant to cure the weakness in Grandma's body. I really felt bad for Grandma since I understood what it was like to want to go home.

Sometimes we just don't get the desires of our heart, do we? Mommy says that God is our Father and He always knows what's best for us. I guess that's just like my daddy. Oh! I just got this terrible thought! If Grandma stays weak in her legs she won't be able to take me for a walk when she keeps me. Goodness! It seems like my mind just wants to run away and I'm having such a hard time catching it.

Does your mind ever run away? Mommy says that she speaks God's word so her mind will stop running. Then she is able to resist the devil and rest in God's arms until she falls asleep. Mommy says we all have the mind of Christ when we accept Him into our hearts.

In the evening I was so restless. It seemed like my body wanted to poopie but just couldn't and the negative thoughts just kept coming until Mommy held me in her arms and spoke God's word until I fell asleep! Hey guys! I'm sure glad Jesus let us have His mind! It really does work! But . . . I wonder what mind Jesus has since He gave His away? Hmm!

Day Five

Oh! No! This was another church day. But something was wrong. I didn't see Daddy and Mommy getting ready. I still didn't feel like drinking any water and still couldn't poopie! Daddy called the hospital where I stayed overnight and they said they would see me. I got all kinds of thoughts in my mind of hiding so they couldn't find me . . . but I felt too weak and tired. Mommy was spending time with God. She opened her Bible to **Psalm 46:10 that says, "Be still and know that I am God!"** She called her precious friend that lives very far away and asked her to pray for direction for them. Last year we visited with them in South Carolina. They had a cat named "Tommy Tucker!" Well, she thought she was the cat's meow. She crawled up on my mommy's lap and hissed at me as though to say, "This is my house and I will be with whomever I want to be with." Well, I wasn't having any of that! After all! Who did she think she was? Didn't she know that dogs always get their cats? My first thought was, "Go get her!" However, I knew that Mommy and Daddy would be upset with me so I gave her the biggest and meanest growl!

You should have seen her back down. Like I said, "Dogs always get their cats!" Daddy and Mommy were really shocked to hear that coming from me. After all, I very rarely bark let alone growl like that! Mommy says that is what we do when we have pent up emotions. I think pent means like when I was stuck in a cage and couldn't get out! Oh! Just the thought of a cage freaks me out! Sometimes something or someone comes along and triggers anger in us and we let them have it! She says this is the result of negative emotions. Well, I have to admit that I saw that green eyed jealousy monster when that cat sat on my mommy's lap. After all, she is my mommy . . . not hers! But . . . Mommy said I had to give the jealousy to God and ask Him to help me. I enjoyed the growl at the time so I guess I may have been holding on to a tiny bit of anger! But now . . . I felt sorry and asked God to forgive me. Great News! He forgave me immediately! Oh! I'm so glad that large weight is off my shoulders! And . . . Tommy Tucker and I didn't have any more problems the rest of our visit! Actually, I think God softened my heart towards her! Imagine that! Opposites can learn to get along!

Well, back to my story! Afterwards, Daddy said, "It's time to go now!" I walked out the front door very slowly and looked at Mommy. She looked at Daddy and said, "Are you sure we are to take Danny over there today? He said, "No, I don't know what to do!" Mommy said, "Well!" When I don't know what to do . . . I do nothing and wait on the Lord."

Mommy and Daddy decided to let the hospital know that we weren't coming today. Mommy told Daddy it was okay for him to go to church and she would stay home with me. Mommy was watching a minister on television that talked about the Jesus prayer and the blind man who kept calling out to Jesus and didn't stop! Then he talked about getting down on our knees and seeking God for the answer. Mommy got down on her knees and cried and sought God for His answer for me. That really makes me sad when Mommy and Daddy cry over me. Normally, when someone cries it makes me feel very sad so I look up into their face and kiss their tears. But I couldn't kiss Mommy's tears that day. I just didn't have the energy!

Later in the evening Mommy was going through some of her journals when a card fell out from her notebook. It said, **"Be still and know that I am God (Psalm 46:10)**. Mommy knew that was her confirmation from God that she and Daddy were to wait since this hospital had not operated on me and didn't know my history! So . . . What is going to happen next?

Day Six

Well, the sun was shining so I got to have my vitamin D. That's what Mommy always says when she sees me taking a sun bath in our dining room. Daddy talked to the veterinarian in the morning and she said to bring me over. I had a little excitement in me to go bye-byes but I still wasn't myself. Mommy had bottled water with her. It was a warm day for February so I looked at the bottle and licked it. Mommy gave me some but I only wanted one sip! Since this was my third day of not drinking any water, the veterinarian put some fluids into me so I wouldn't be dehydrated. I'm not sure I understand that word but I sure felt dry inside. Mommy says that people can be dehydrated in the Lord when they don't drink of His living water every day. I really don't understand why she calls it living water. I never knew that water could be dead! Well, anyway I have so much to learn!

The veterinarian also gave me some medication for colitis and gastronitis. All I knew was I must have a lot of itis's! Mommy told me she had a retreat for a church and the theme was **Sinitis!** I don't know if that's what I have or not? Mommy said that God gave her that word and it's not in the dictionary. Actually, you wouldn't believe how many words God gives Mommy and she has to look them up in the dictionary! Mommy gets a lot of excitement in her spirit when God does that! Well, Mommy says that all things work together for good to those that love the Lord. So . . . . would you believe we found out that my red blood cell count was up thirty per cent more since the surgery so that helped to put us all at ease! But . . . I still didn't want to eat and drink on my own so Daddy and Mommy were force feeding me and using a dropper to get water into me again. I heard Grandma say that I was getting even and liked being pampered by Mommy and Daddy for making me go through the surgery. I don't understand that word pampered since I hate wearing pampers! Well, actually, don't tell Mommy and Daddy . . . but I really felt that I could get use to all this great attention!

Beginning to Heal-Day Seven

Mommy says that God told her this one day, "There is beauty in the midst of darkness!" She said God placed a beautiful blue jay right in front of her as she was walking. Well, I guess that's true since we got some good news. The veterinarian's office called and said the biopsy showed no cancer in me! Praise God! I don't ever have to deal with this again! However, Mommy and Daddy were still force feeding me and putting water through a dropper in my mouth. Mommy says when her emotions want to run away she stops them with God's Word. God told Mommy again to be still and know that He is God. He said, "I started the work and I will accomplish it. Trust Me!" Then I heard Mommy sing again and praise God! Also, I did have a little more energy but no appetite or thirst!

The next day Daddy told Mommy to call the veterinarian and let her know what was going on with me. She told Mommy that I might be having problems with some acid in my stomach and she would need to purchase Pepcid AC and give it to me. I never heard of that before but people take that too! Well, in the evening Daddy and Mommy were giving me water in a dropper again. Every time Daddy would give me water in a dropper he would put a bowl of water in front of me to entice me to drink. Every day I had been turning it down. However, something was taking place in me and I began to feel thirsty! Guess I was thirsty for that living water since it sure didn't taste dead to me. Boy! It felt great to thirst again! Mommy lifted up her hands to the Lord and praised and thanked

Him! Daddy and Mommy were so excited to see me drinking again on my own.

Oh! By the way! Did you know the number seven in the Bible represents healing? Imagine that . . . God healed me on the seventh day after surgery! Don't tell Daddy and Mommy but . . . . I knew that I could no longer have all this attention so . . . I had to give it up. It was good while it lasted but something in me knew that I needed more water in me since I was really beginning to feel dry inside! Mommy says that's what happens to people when God's presence is drawing them. They begin to feel dry and thirsty for His living water! Do you feel dry inside? Are you thirsty for His living water?

One Month after Surgery

Well, it's been one month since the surgery and I'm behaving like a little puppy. Well, not in all areas but I certainly have so much more energy. I run and play with my toys and love when Daddy or Mommy chases me. Every day we thank God for the blessing of giving me a longer life. It's hard to believe that I even went through the surgery. You can hardly see any scars since I am so healed. Mommy says that's what happens to people when Jesus heals them. They aren't scarred for life. We don't really know why I had a ruptured spleen. However; about six months before I had gotten ill, I thought I was walking into Daddy and Mommy's bedroom instead I walked downstairs. I tumbled down some of the carpeted steps but got up very quickly and didn't even cry. Actually, my ego was bruised more than I was. Daddy checked me over thoroughly. I didn't even let out a whimper when he touched me. Daddy and Mommy realized because my eyesight had gotten worse, they had to place a baby gate at the entrance of the steps at night.

We all learned a lot of lessons with me being sick. God promised to never leave or forsake us . . . . that's what my grandma says. Then she says, "I need you now!" Wow! I believe God loves to hear that since some people treat Him like the Maytag repair man . . . . he never has any appliances to fix. Sometimes we try to fix ourselves and let God out of the picture. Well, I'm so glad Daddy and Mommy didn't let God out of the picture. You see, God has so much more for my life than I even know. Speaking of my life . . . . I believe God wants to heal my eyes since God told

Mommy to take authority over the curse of blindness in me. Will you believe with us for my eyesight? If so, please let me know that you will believe God with us for a miracle!

May I just speak very frank with you today? God is not a "plop, plop, fizz, fizz, oh what a relief it is" God. You and I need His peace and comfort in the midst of a chaotic world. Mommy says that God is our friend and sticks closer than a brother. Do you see Him that way in your life? Or . . . Do you just call on Him when you are in trouble or do you talk to Him about everything every day?

Maybe some of you haven't asked Jesus into your heart. God has a great plan and purpose for your life. You are not a mistake! You are created by God to do His works and are wonderfully and fearfully made by Him. If you haven't asked Him into your heart, please pray this prayer with me.

Lord, I confess that I am a sinner. I ask that you forgive me of my sins and come into my heart today and cleanse my heart and mind. I believe in you and no longer want to be in control of my life. I ask you to be Lord of every area of my life in Jesus' Name. Amen.

Wow! Since you have asked Jesus into your heart, are you ready to go on a love walk with Him? I thank God every day for the life He has given me. I really got a rough start but God led me to the best Mommy and Daddy a guy could ever have. He sure has been taking me on an exciting journey! Mommy says He is always ahead of us and is our rear guard to protect us. Wow! With protection like that how can we be afraid?

Well, God has been using me as His vessel to teach my mommy many lessons. So . . . I'm going to teach you to the best of my ability more lessons from Danny. Yep! That's me!

God's Pep Talk

One morning I came running into the house shivering from the frigid temperature outside! Brrr! Even with my sweater on, I was really cold! Mommy picked me up and wrapped me into a blanket and held me in her arms. Boy! Did I love that! As Mommy continued to hold me, my mouth stopped quivering and I began to relax in her arms. She looked me in the eyes and began to tell me how much she loved me. She called me her little brown eyed blonde and spoke gentle words to me. Of course! I couldn't resist those words so I began to give her lots of loving kisses. Mommy looked me in the eyes and said, "Mommy gives you a pep talk every day, doesn't she?

I didn't understand what a pep talk was but I loved being cuddled and cherished by Mommy. Actually, I thought of it as being a pet talk since I'm her favorite pet! Mommy says that a pep talk is a brief vigorous talk meant to inspire! Well, believe me I was really getting inspired to get down on the floor, pick up my toys and run all around the house. Mommy said she realized that God has inspiration for us as we study His Word and spend time in His presence daily. God's written and spoken Word to us is His Pep Talk! I don't know about you but I sure don't want to miss out on Mommy's pet talk daily so why would you want to miss out on God's Pep Talk?

Some people say they are just too busy to spend time with God. Mommy says that she always prays, "Lord, don't let me get too busy that I won't have time for you!" You see Mommy knows that if she is too busy for God she won't be able to accomplish His plan for her life because she is too busy performing her own plans!

John 3:16 says, "For God so dearly and greatly prized the world that He even gave up His only begotten son (unique son), so that whoever believes in (trusts in, clings to, relies on) Him shall not perish (come to destruction, be lost) but have eternal (everlasting life)" (AMP)

Do you know how special you are? Most of us don't. Mommy says it has taken her years of getting renewed in her heart and mind. I think she means as she spends time reading God's Word and receives His pep talk; it enables her to give that negative "Stinkin' Thinkin'" over to Him! As a result her efforts cause a breakout of her emotions that lead to breakthroughs in her life! Mommy says this is God's Profound Empowerment Plan for His children! In other words, God's plan requires thoughtful study of His Word that brings power and authority which enables you to no longer have low self esteem but wear God's shoes of confidence! God already worked His plan out in advance for your life. It's a matter of you following in His footsteps!

Think of this! Your great Awesome Daddy God dearly loves and prizes you. In other words, He values you highly! He paid the price to have you for His prize! Hey guys! Do you know what this means? It means you are not a mistake! You were placed here by God. He wants you to hear His heart for you today. You are precious in His sight.

Can I be frank with you? As I was shivering from the cold, many of you are shivering from the coldness in your heart that has come from the pain in your past. Jesus wants to pick you up and wrap you in His blanket of love! One morning Mommy was noticing many icicles hanging over the door. They were so big that it didn't look like anything would ever be able to penetrate through them. However, later in the afternoon the sun was shining as she watched the icicles beginning to melt. Mommy said the Holy Spirit spoke in her insides. He said, "Many of my children have icicles in their heart! Brrr! I don't know about you but I don't like being cold and certainly don't want to feel it in my heart! Mommy says that God's Sonshine will melt the coldest of hearts.

I am reminded of a day Daddy gave me a biscuit. Daddy had a piece of toast spread with butter and jelly that looked much better to me. I spit that old biscuit out of my mouth hoping Daddy would give me some of his toast. Mommy and Daddy thought I looked really funny! Of course, my daddy gave me some of his toast. Oh! It was so . . . good! You see . . . if I would have held on to that old biscuit, I would never have enjoyed Daddy's toast!

So . . . what fleshly food do you need to spit out of your mouth today to receive your Daddy God's spiritual food? No matter what you have experienced in your past or what you are going through now, Jesus is here to speak life to you. Give Him your victim mentality and pick up His Word that is your Victory! C'mon! Let's do this together!

Lord, forgive me for holding onto the past and remaining a victim of (unforgiveness, jealousy, fear, worry and so forth) Take this coldness out of my heart so I can feel your blanket of love wrapped around me. Show me where I am too busy to spend time with you. I give you low self esteem and receive your shoes of confidence. Thank you for the victory that has already been won by you in Jesus' Name. Amen

Wow! Can you feel those cold icicles beginning to melt in God's Sonshine?

Go Jesus! Go Jesus! Go Jesus!

Go Jesus! Go Jesus! Go Jesus! In my heart . . . In my mind . . . In my soul! Go Jesus! Go Jesus! Go Jesus! Oh! My goodness! That feels so . . . . good! I love to cheer with Mommy!

Mommy says time really flies quickly when she is cheering for Jesus. I'm not sure what she means by that. I never saw time have wings and take off like birds. Boy! People say the funniest things! And . . . where is Jesus anyway? If we are cheering for Him don't you think He would show up? Mommy says we need to lift up the Name of Jesus everyday! She says when she speaks His Name . . . she feels her spirit being recharged by His presence in her heart and mind and soul! Well, evidently Jesus must stay only in your insides. The only one I ever saw getting recharged was the energizer bunny on television. Now, I must admit I do really get a burst of energy when my daddy comes home. But I see Daddy with my own eyes. Mommy doesn't see Jesus with her natural eyes and yet she gets a burst of energy from Him.

Jeremiah 24:7 says, "And I will give them a heart to know, recognize, understand and be acquainted with me that I am the Lord; and they will be my people, and I will be their God, for they will return to me with their whole heart." (AMP)

Boy! He must be really a very important person since Mommy says He is everywhere and knows everything!

I'm sure some of you have wondered why every message on the Promise Land Ministries blog podcast begins with Go Jesus! Well, Mommy and the Promise Land Ministries team had a women's weekend retreat. The first morning Mommy woke up at 6:00 A.M. sitting on her bed doing a cheer for Jesus. Two of the women had roomed with her. Mommy was so excited that she called one of the ladies over to see the cheer the Holy Spirit had given her. This precious lady wasn't quite awake and asked, "Is it morning yet?" Mommy showed her the cheer for Jesus and they began cheering together. I don't know about you but I'm not a morning guy and really wouldn't appreciate all that noise so early! The other precious lady said, "What are you two doing?" Mommy said all three of them started singing and cheering for Jesus! Mommy says she really isn't an early morning gal but God gives her supernatural energy during the retreats and renewals!

Well, that day was filled with excitement and passion as they all shouted out cheers for Jesus!

So . . . how about you . . . are you shouting out cheers for Jesus or are you hiding under the covers like I do in the morning? Mommy says Jesus wants us to cheer for Him every day or the rocks will cry out to Him.

Now . . . I really don't understand that! Whoever heard of rocks talking? What in the world does that mean? I don't know about you but I'm sure feeling confused again. Sometimes I just shake my ears since I can't figure it all out.

Mommy says we need to look at God's Word to understand this.

> **Luke 19:35-37 says, "And they brought it to Jesus; then they threw their garments over the colt and set Jesus upon it. And as He rode along, the people kept spreading their garments on the road. As He was approaching (the city), at the descent of the Mount of Olives, the whole crowd of the disciples began to rejoice and to praise God (extolling Him exultantly and) loudly for all the**

mighty miracles *and* works of power that they had witnessed."(AMP)

Wow! Can you picture this scene with me? They had witnessed many miracles with their natural eyes. Jesus turned the water into wine at a wedding, healed the lepers, gave sight to the blind and healed the crippled that caused them to throw their crutches down and walk again. He even raised a man who was pronounced dead and cast out demonic spirits. Shouts began to be heard everywhere as the people rolled out the red carpet and celebrated Jesus with their praises!

Luke 19:38 says, "Crying, Blessed (celebrated with praises) is the King, Who comes in the name of the Lord! Peace in heaven (freedom there from all the distresses that are experienced as the result of sin) and glory (majesty and splendor) in the highest (heaven)!" (AMP)

Wow! Can you imagine the party they were having for Jesus? I would have loved to have been invited! Did you catch this? Jesus gives us freedom from all distresses that are experienced as a result of sin. Nobody on this earth has the power to free you like Jesus did!

Well, as usual the religious leaders didn't like all the noise the crowd was making so they told Jesus to get his disciples under control. But . . . Jesus loved all the praises and told them if people don't praise Him the earth won't be able to keep silent!

"And some of the Pharisees from the throng said to Jesus, Teacher, reprove your disciples!
He replied, I tell you that if these keep silent, the very stones will cry out." (Luke 19:39-40 AMP)

Mommy said she used to know God as a Bible God. However, she knows Him as her personal God which causes her to shout praises to Him every day. Do you recognize Jesus as your personal friend or are you afraid to get close to Him? Mommy says, "If you grab hold of the love of your Heavenly Father, you would truly grab hold of the love that He has for you and for each other!"

Maybe you know Him as a Bible God like Mommy did. I'm going to ask you to pray this with me.:

> **Thank you, Lord. You have given me a heart to know, recognize and understand and be acquainted with you. I want to love you with my whole heart, soul and mind. Help me to set my mind on you and not on what is going on around me. I shout praises to my King in Jesus' Name! Amen.**

Are you ready to be a cheerleader for Jesus? Let's give Him a shout of acclamation and give Him a standing ovation which brings joy, gladness, and encouragement into your heart and mind today! No one deserves any higher praise than Jesus!

C'mon! It's a new morning! Let's shout together like you really mean it! **Go Jesus! Go Jesus! Go Jesus! In my heart . . . . In my mind . . . . In my soul!** Way to go guys!

Who's in the driver's seat?

Mommy needed to run some errands one day and decided to take me along. Oh! How I love to go by byes! I always run out to the car, jump in and sit up very proudly like I'm the dawg! No, I didn't misspell the word dawg. In other words, I'm the cool dude! Well, it was great traveling with Mommy but I was getting tired of being cooped up and was ready to stretch my legs! On the way home, I started getting anxious to go home and began jumping from the front seat to the back seat. Mommy said, "Danny, you don't have to worry. Mommy has everything under control!"

One day Mommy and Daddy were traveling to a church in another county and were running late. She started to get anxious with many thoughts racing through her mind. They were supposed to meet a lady that Mommy hadn't seen for many years. Mommy was concerned that the lady would think they weren't coming. Did you notice the word . . . concern? Mommy says the word concern sounds better than worry since most Christians don't like to admit they are worried. Actually, when you look up the word concern, it means Worry! Boy! They talk about us pets and how silly we are. I think people can be very silly! Why don't they just admit they are worried and give it to their Daddy God so He can put peace in their heart?

Well, Mommy was starting to get very worried and was talking to God! The Holy Spirit spoke in her insides, "Sit back . . . relax . . . and enjoy the scenery!

Philippians 4:6 says, "Do not be anxious about anything but in every circumstance and in everything by prayer and petition (definite requests) with thanksgiving continue to make your wants known to God!" (AMP)

When Mommy stopped looking at her watch but focused on God's spoken word, she began to actually enjoy the scenery. She no longer had anxious thoughts about my daddy's driving and being late but allowed God to be in the driver's seat of her mind and emotions!

Isaiah 26:3 says, "You will guard him and keep him in perfect peace whose mind (both its inclination and its character is stayed on you because he commits himself to you, leans on you and hopes confidently in you." (AMP)

So . . . Is your mind on Jesus today instead of all the circumstances and people? Are you reclining in your seat to incline your ear to hear God's word for you? When Mommy leaned back in her seat and committed the day to Jesus and trusted that He was taking care of everything, she received His peace! By the way, the lady Mommy and Daddy were supposed to meet, was delayed too! What an awesome God!

Maybe you have been in the driver's seat for so long that you don't know how to move over and let Jesus take the wheel!

Say this with me . . . Thank you Jesus for guarding me and keeping me in perfect peace because my mind is on you. My heart is opened to receive your Word for all my circumstances and challenges that I meet. I commit myself to you, lean on and confidently hope in you today! I give you complete control of my life in Jesus' Name. Amen.

Hey Guys . . . God has amazing days ahead of you. You don't have to worry or fret. Your Daddy God has everything under control! If you have been in the driver's seat . . . MOVE OVER!!! **Sit back, relax** and **enjoy the scenery** that God has for you today!

This is the life!

Where's the beef?

One day Mommy sat down to eat lunch which consisted of a ham and cheese sandwich, chips and a diet drink. Not the most nutritious lunch, is it? However, I kept begging Mommy for a bite. Actually, I just wanted the meat but Mommy wouldn't give it to me. She gave me a chip and I turned up my nose in strong resistance. Mommy said, "Danny, you're holding out for the meat, aren't you?" I definitely was holding out for the meat and kept resisting the junk food.

So . . . are you eating the meat of God's WORD and resisting the junk food in your mind and emotions or are you gobbling down the junk food and resisting the meat of God's WORD? Mommy said years ago a fast food restaurant had a sign on their window that read, "Where's the beef?" They were advertising that their sandwiches were packed with lots of beef. They said the other places had very little beef in their sandwich.

The Bible is packed with lots of meat for your spirit. Daddy loves to sink his teeth into the delicacy of a big juicy steak. Mommy says when she reads God's Word daily; she sinks her teeth into the delicacy of His WORD! Just as you choose food daily for nourishment to your body, you must choose God's food for your spiritual nourishment. Instead of choosing foods that make you feel sluggish and eventually cause health problems, you need to choose foods that help you to be more alert, energetic and make your bones stronger! Mommy says you have a choice to feed your flesh and allow the negativity to remain which cause a depressed state in your emotions or . . . . feed your spirit with God's WORD which cause your spirit to rise up and be strong with His power and encouragement! Well, I don't mind telling you that I sure didn't understand what feeding the flesh meant. I don't feed my flesh . . . I feed my mouth! After all, my skin can't taste any food. And . . . . how in the world can you feed your insides with God's Word in the Bible? I don't know about you but I'm not into eating paper from a book! Boy! Sometimes all this learning can be very confusing! Well, this is how Mommy explained it to me. She said, "Danny, sometimes you want to eat food that isn't good for you. And . . . your mind says, "I want it!" and your emotions follow your mind. However, when you remember what Mommy told you about certain foods that can make you really sick you can choose to continue thinking of what you want or what is good for you! It's your choice!

Job 36:16 says, "He is wooing you from the jaws of distress, to a spacious place free from restriction to the comfort of your table laden with choice food." (NIV)

Are you going through an affliction that has placed you into a restriction? Are you sitting in a dark room of negativity and catering to your flesh? Cater means to provide for the gratification of any needs or food. Sometimes I want to cater to the smell of food that isn't good for me and might make me sick so I have to choose to think about the consequences instead of my own desires. Believe me, I can feel quite distressed if I continue to think about food that smells so . . . . good. However, I begin to settle down in my mind when I take Mommy at her word and focus on what food is good for me. Now . . . do you understand?

When you spend time in God's presence and read His Word, He will free you from the distress of life. You will no longer be limited or confined in your mind catering to the needs of your flesh such as doubt, worry, anxiousness, guilt, fear or discouragement.

> **Psalm 119:147 says, "I anticipated the dawning of the morning and cried in childlike prayer. I hoped in your word." (AMP)**

Through God's Word served daily, we are no longer under the enemy's restrictions but receive the prescription for God's truth that causes us to anticipate the dawning of each morning with hope in our heart.

> **Close your eyes with me. Now . . . imagine God taking you out of this dark area in your life as you say this with me. Thank you, Lord for wooing me from the jaws of distress to a spacious place free from restriction to the comfort of your table laden with choice food. I have cried out to you and now look forward to each morning waking up with hope in my heart because I have hope in your Word for me today in Jesus' Name. Amen.**

Wow! God shined His light on the dark area of selfishness in my heart today. I didn't realize that I was being selfish. I feel so good when I allow God to free me! What dark area did He shine His light on in your heart?

God's invisible fence!

So . . . let's talk about fear! Every time Daddy turns on the television I hear a lot of terrible things that really hurt me. Sometimes I see Mommy crying when she sees so many people in pain and suffering. Mommy really has a tender heart for God's children. She says that she feels God's heart hurting too! Did you know that when you cry out to God . . . He hears your cries? One day Mommy was taking me for a walk. As we walked in front of a house, two large dogs came running as though to attack me. Believe it or not! I wasn't intimidated by the larger dogs that were growling, snarling and showing their teeth. I kept my position and didn't cower in fear or put my tail between my legs and run. Actually, I knew my mommy would protect me. They were coming straight for me when suddenly they stopped in their tracks. I looked at Mommy and she said, "It's okay, Danny! There is an invisible fence around the house!" The dogs knew how far they could go without being shocked by the fence.

Mommy said one day she was going through a strong battle in her mind and emotions because of a situation that she was going through. God gave her a vision of a no trespassing sign on her property. He said, "When you asked me into your heart . . . you became my property. I have placed a hedge around you that the enemy cannot penetrate."

In the first part of Job 1:10 satan was speaking to God about his servant, Job, saying, **"Have you not put a hedge about him and his house and all that he has, on every side?"** Hedge

40

means to shut in for formation, protection or restraint or a fence. When I saw those dogs barking, growling and showing their teeth, I knew my mommy would protect me. So . . . let me ask you this question. Is the devil growling and showing his teeth to you today?

Psalm 91:9-11 says, "Because God is my refuge, the High God my very own home, evil can't get close to me, harm can't get through the door. He ordered His angels to guard me wherever I go." (The Message)

Mommy says that she used to be grounded and rooted in fear instead of rooted and grounded in God's love. **I John 4:18 says, "Perfect love casts out fear!"** You see, she now knows how much God loves her. When God was pulling the root of fear out of Mommy she had to give God her running shoes in order to receive God's slippers of rest! You see I knew my mommy loved me and would protect me. Even though I felt afraid, I stood my position as Daddy and Mommy's little guy!

We all experience the emotions of fear sometimes in our life. But . . . when we know how much God loves us and who we are in Him, we are able to stand and take our position. When you see in your mind a no trespassing sign, the enemy won't be able to get through the door of your mind and emotions. So . . . do you have your running shoes on or have you given them to God? I don't know about you, but I really get tired running. I love to just rest in my Daddy's arms!

Are you resting in your Daddy God's arms, wearing His slippers of rest? If not, will you say this prayer with me?

Thank you, Lord! You have a hedge over me, my household and all my possessions on every side. You are a shield for me and the glory and the lifter of my head. Because you are my refuge, the High God, my very own home, evil can't get close to me and harm can't get through the door of my mind and emotions. You have

ordered your angels to guard me wherever I go therefore, I am not afraid of anything the enemy will try to bring my way through circumstances or people today in Jesus' Name! Amen.

Wow! Can you feel faith in your insides rising?

Are you in a tug of war?

One morning Mommy decided to play with me. I grabbed my toy bone and wouldn't let her have it. Mommy and I began playing tug of war with my bone. She kept trying to take it out of my mouth and said, "Danny, how bad do you want this?" I thought, "I'll show you how bad I want this!" As Mommy kept trying to pull my bone out of my mouth, I held it so tight that she couldn't release it. I continued clenching my teeth on the bone and growling. Of course, it was a playful growl! After all, I wouldn't think of giving a mean growl to anyone. Well, that's not exactly true. Sometimes my friend Alfie comes to see me. He is a little white Westiepoo. Mommy says we look so cute together but I'll let you be the judge of that. He's my little friend next door but sometimes he gets too aggressive and I have to growl at him to stop! Well, Mommy suddenly realized this is what God wants us to do. He wants us to hold onto His promises like I was holding onto my bone and didn't let go! In other words, God wants us to be aggressive and not allow satan to be the aggressor!

Did you ever see a bull dog holding onto a bone? Now mind you, a bull dog is more ferocious than I am. Mommy can take food out of my mouth if I'm not supposed to have it. One day I grabbed a treat before supper and she came along and took it right out of my mouth! I was so stunned and didn't realize where my treat had gone. Mommy told me that it would spoil my supper so I had to wait until after the meal. Well, I don't think you could do that with most bull dogs. Mommy says God wants us to have that **Bull**

Dog Faith that is bold, aggressive and courageous in the midst of our trials. When satan pulls out his tools of discouragement in our minds and emotions we need to clench our teeth and hold fast to our faith in God!

Hebrews 11: 6 says, "But without faith it is impossible to please *and* be satisfactory to Him. For whoever would come near to God must (necessarily) believe that God exists and that He is the rewarder of those who earnestly *and* diligently seek Him (out)." (AMP)

Is satan trying to steal your faith today? Maybe you are in a situation that God is saying, "Hold on" and you are saying, "This is too hard!" Maybe you have been waiting many years for your promises to manifest and are saying, "How long, Lord?" Hold On! Your Daddy God loves you and will give you His best. Are you diligently seeking Him? The Greek meaning for diligently is to inquire, desire, endeavor, worship!

Do you desire more of God or are you focused on God answering your problems? Mommy says that she has been waiting for some promises from God for many years. One day she began to clench her teeth on the problem and not the promise! Satan was playing tug of war with her mind and emotions. God showed her that it was her choice! He wanted her to look to Him who is the solution to all her problems. Was she going to have **Bull Dog Faith** to believe God's Word or Chicken Little fear? Chicken Little fear is an alarmist who warns of imaginary danger and always thinks something bad is going to happen! Now . . . I ask you! Would you rather have a **bull dog** on your side or *Chicken Little*? Whoa! I don't know about you . . . but I sure want the **Bull Dog Faith** over having *Chicken Little fear*!

So . . . have you been playing tug of war with God or the enemy? Is your focus on your problems or on God who loves you with an everlasting love, supplies all of your needs and promises to never leave or forsake you? Mommy says she has a thank you list to God. Every day she writes on her list what she is thankful for and expresses her thanks to God. She says this not only pleases God but she feels surrounded by His love, peace and joy! I don't know about you but I think that's a great idea!

> **Say this with me. Thank you, Lord. I am not alone in this trial for your promise is to never leave or forsake me. Thank you for supplying all of my needs and for loving me even when I begin to doubt your promises in Jesus' Name! Amen.**

Don't look at what you don't have but thank God for all that you do have. You will be amazed how your spirit will soar. He will take you to higher heights of faith and trust in Him than you could ever think or imagine!

I can't wait to write my thank you list today! Will you join me?

God's Special Delivery

Mommy had written a book under the inspiration of the Holy Spirit. No, I didn't say perspiration although she said there were so many challenges in writing and publishing her first book, "Touch Me". Do you know the saying, "Genius is ten percent inspiration and 90 per cent perspiration?" Well, Mommy says it's one hundred per cent inspiration with the Holy Spirit since He is the genius! However, our minds have to be continually renewed with God's Word so we don't excrete fear, worry and anxiety! Every day Mommy waited to receive her first copy of her book that was in the printing department. She felt like she was sitting on pins and needles waiting with great expectation for the book to arrive. I don't know about you but I certainly wouldn't be excited about sitting on pins and needles. Ouch! That would really hurt! Oh! Well! I'm still trying to understand people, after all God made them too!

As Mommy thought about the excitement in receiving the finished book, she realized this is how God wants us to wait for delivery of His Word daily. She says when she opens up God's Word she expects to receive His encouragement. So . . . are you waiting with great expectation? Are you watching for His mail to be delivered? After all, God has a love letter for you every day. Mommy says she anticipates what God wants to say daily! I think she means that she eagerly looks forward to hearing God's wisdom for her situations. When Mommy retrieves her mail she doesn't know what is in it unless she opens it up.

You have that choice too! God has written and finished His love letter for you but it's up to you to open His mail. So . . . why are many of God's children not opening their mail? Maybe you are too busy and the busyness of life is taking precedence over spending time with God. Or maybe you feel so tired that it's hard to get up off that couch of depression. Whatever the reason is . . . it's time to read God's mail for you daily. Don't let everything pile up and sit on the table of discouragement. I love to haul the mail as my daddy calls it. When I am sitting on the couch feeling lonely, since Mommy and Daddy are too busy to sit with me, suddenly Daddy says, "Come on Danny, "It's time to haul the mail!" I immediately jump off the couch with great excitement in knowing that I am going to go outside and walk with my daddy. Are you excited to walk with your Daddy God? Are you ready to get up off that couch and stop allowing the enemy to keep you bound in depression? Come on . . . let's get excited over God's Word! As Mommy's book came by special delivery, God has a **Special Delivery** for you today!

I can hear some of you saying, "It's been so long since I've checked my mail that I've forgotten where to look." Or maybe some of you are saying, "I know there is lots of mail but I've been too busy and now it's piled up and collecting dust. I'm too overwhelmed and don't know where to begin!"

Psalm 55:22 and I Peter 5:7 tells us to cast our cares which are anxieties, worries and concerns on the Lord and He will sustain you; He will never let the righteous fall.

The definition of cast is to discard, reject, to throw or dismiss. Notice . . . **you** must discard and reject the negative thoughts first! In other words, stop accepting those words from the enemy that sap strength from your life and leave you tired and worn out from your circumstances.

> Psalm 62:5 says, "My soul, wait only upon God and silently submit to Him; for my hope and expectation are from Him." (AMP)

In the **Message version it says, "God, the one and only. I'll wait as long as He says, everything I hope for comes from Him, so why not? He's solid rock under my feet, breathing room for my soul, an impregnable castle. I'm set free for life!"**

Hmmm! I wonder if impregnable is like being pregnant. *Mommy says, "As we open God's love letter and breathe in His presence, we become pregnant with God's Word of Hope that drives out the negative emotions that makes room for His peace, love and joy! As we are in this waiting period we develop security in Him and let go of our insecurities. We begin to wait with great expectation for the delivery of His Word that overcomes all the challenges. God's Word begins to grow inside of us that began with a tiny seed of hope. God's Words of Hope begin to grow bigger and the discouragement becomes smaller. Finally, the day of delivery is here! God's living water has become so full that it begins to overflow. We have experienced a break out of emotions and now it's time for the break through! God has brought the long awaited promises that change our lives completely!" It's time for the celebration!*

Did you catch that? Wow! Are you willing to wait on God's timing and place all of your expectations at His feet? Think of this! You are set for life! He is your solid rock when everything around you is crumbling. If you have accepted Jesus into your heart you have His Holy Spirit within you that enables you to be an overcomer. When you face trials and tribulations you have His courage and power within to stand firm and not be shaken. You are immune to satan's attacks and your soul can freely breathe in God's peace and not be constricted by the enemy's lies.

> **James 4:7 says, "Submit yourselves, then, to God. Resist the devil, and he will flee from you." (NIV)**

Notice . . . when you give these negative thoughts of worry, anxiousness, fear and discouragement to the Lord you submit to God's Word. The Holy Spirit enables you to reject the enemy's words that bring discouragement.

Hey Guys . . . . God has already written your story and has a great plan for you! God loves you so much. Just as I love to walk with my daddy every day, Your Daddy God desires for you to walk with Him by reading His love letter for you.

May I encourage you to lay your burdens at Jesus feet today? Give Him all your worries, anxieties and fears. Open up God's Word for you. God has His Special Delivery that contains His message that will bring deliverance in your life!

If you are feeling discouraged, may I ask you to pray this with me:

Lord, I confess that I have been worried, anxious and fearful (tell God in your own words your circumstances). I give these burdens today. I reject these thoughts of negativity for I no longer believe the enemy's words over *Your Word*! Thank you for delivering me from discouragement today. I am an over comer from satan's lies and unable to be shaken by his attacks in Jesus Name. Amen!

Take a deep breath and breathe in His peace for you today! Now . . . go to your mailbox with great expectation and pick up His **Special Delivery** for you today!

Do you have a hopeful expectancy?

My daddy left for a mission's trip to Texas with the pastor and some other men from the church. I don't mind telling you that I was quite upset. First of all, I don't understand why he had to go to Texas to minister when he could minister in his own back yard. After all, I need all of his attention and I'm not very happy when I don't receive it. Actually, I think Daddy felt bad about not taking me along but just like the pastor doesn't allow me to come to church, I bet the mean old pastor said no dogs allowed! Sorry! I get a little fired up when I think of the whole situation and my emotions start to run away! I sat on the couch in front of our living room window waiting for his return. Now just to give you an idea of how much I love to sit at the window and look out, Mommy used to have blinds at the window which caused me not to have full view. One day she decided the blinds needed to come down so I could see out! Boy! How is that for wrapping my mommy and daddy around my little paw?

Well, every time a car came close to our house, I would jump up at the window and get really excited. However, as I watched the cars pass by our house my head went down. Every day I continued to watch for my daddy. As the days went by I started to feel really sad and gloomy. No, I didn't say looney! Although, every day that my daddy didn't come home, I felt like I was going crazy with fear that he would never come back. One day Mommy received a phone call from her friend. As she was talking with her, she realized that I looked like her friend felt! Mommy realized that I didn't have the hope of my daddy coming back but her friend had the promise of her Daddy God never leaving or forsaking her!

So . . . even though I was feeling forsaken by my daddy . . . I was. But Mommy and her friend had a promise from their Daddy God!

> **Matthew 28:20 that says, "Teaching them to observe everything that I have commanded you, and behold, I am with you all the days (perpetually, uniformly, and on every occasion), to the (very) close *and* consummation of the age." *(AMP)* Amen (so let it be)**

Perpetually means continuing, lasting forever, unlimited amount of time. The definition of Uniformly is agreeing or identical with each other.

In other words, your Daddy God is continually identifying with you in every trial that you are going through and perfecting those areas in you to bring about His completion that will last forever. Think of this! God whom we can barely describe the capacity of His love in our minds humbles Himself to have fellowship with you!

> **Psalm 42:11 says, "Why are you downcast O my inner self?" And why should you moan over me and be disquieted within me? Hope in God and wait expectantly for Him for I shall yet praise Him. Who is the help of my countenance and my God?" (AMP)**

The psalmist was expressing his emotions in the midst of the difficult circumstances yet he remained in faith and was waiting with great expectation in praise while placing His hope in God!

Mommy said she was watching a television show called Seventh Heaven. Rev. Camden and his wife's little girl; Ruthie was upset because her teacher called her stupid. As a result she wasn't working up to the capacity that she normally did in class because her thoughts were on getting out of the class. Her parents went to the principal and he came up with an idea to send Ruthie to a private school that only very bright children could attend. When her parents told her she could leave the class, she was excited and said, "Thanks God!" However, when she found out about leaving the school, not just the class room, she lifted her hands up and said, "Why have you forsaken me?"

Perhaps you have been expressing your emotions to others but have lost hope that God will rescue you in the midst of pain and suffering in your life.

> **Mark 11:23 says, "Truly I tell you, whoever says to this mountain, Be lifted up and thrown into the sea and does not doubt at all in his heart but believes that what he says will take place, it will be done for him." (AMP)**

Now we all know that we can't begin to lift up a mountain. That's really a no brainer! So . . . what does this mean? Well, I'll try to explain this since Mommy talks about this a lot in her ministry. Mommy says that many of us speak negative words about our problems instead of speaking to the mountain that contains the problems. Some of you may be saying, "I've prayed for my spouse's salvation for over twenty years and it hasn't happened. He/she still continues ignoring God's plan for their life. God's promises don't give a length of time to accomplish His plan and purpose for our life. Whether you have children taking the wrong road to addictions, lost loved ones through death or divorce, experienced betrayal of a Christian friend, or are going through a financial crisis . . . God's Word remains the same! He is a God of the Impossible!

Those days without my daddy were really hard for me. Don't get me wrong . . . I love my mommy too but she just isn't my daddy! Now there was a happy ending to this story! My daddy did return. However, your Daddy God has never left you even though you may feel like He has! So . . . are you expressing your emotions to your Daddy God and allowing Him to shine His light in the darkness of your heart? Do you need wisdom, direction, peace, joy, and most of all His love for yourself and others?

> **Close your eyes and say this with me. Thank you, Lord. You never leave or forsake me. Forgive me for losing hope in you and what you can accomplish in and through me. I give you these problems (name them) that are impossible for me to solve. You are the God of the Impossible so I place my faith and confidence in you. I wait with great expectation for you to show yourself strong in my life today for nothing is impossible for you in Jesus' Name. Amen.**

Don't you just love happy endings!

God delights in you!

One day Mommy decided to teach me some commands with my ball. She would pick up my ball and throw it for me to fetch. After I caught it in my mouth, she expected me to sit down and drop the ball onto the floor. In the beginning I didn't quite understand but I soon caught on to what she was saying. When I obeyed her commands, I received a delicious treat! However, there were times that I didn't want to give up the ball so I would hold onto it, run away from her and play with it all by myself.

Mommy said she would sit down and watch my playful antics all the while patiently waiting for me to drop the ball. I'm not sure what **antics** are but I sure hope it's not like **ticks**! One time Mommy and Daddy and I went for a walk in the woods. You should have seen Mommy. She was really scared and kept looking for snakes and bears. Daddy just kept on trucking up the path with me on a leash like he didn't have a care in the world. As for me, I was happy to be going for a walk with my two favorite people! Afterwards, Mommy found four ticks on me and removed them immediately. I'm sure glad she checked me for ticks. Always remember when you walk in the woods, ticks can get on you too. Oops! Sorry! I got off the path that we started walking! Hmmm! I think that is called a rabbit trail . . . although I didn't see any rabbits! Now where was I? Oh! Yeah!

One day Mommy heard the Lord say, "I delight in you today!" Mommy's heart was so touched that she began to cry. Her first thought was, "How can you be delighted in me?" I messed up again!" She heard Him say in her insides, "You have a heart for me!" God wasn't looking at her mess ups. He was delighted that she is His child and would help her clean up the messes in her life.

> **Numbers 14:8 says, "If the Lord delights in us, then He will bring us into this land and give it to us, a land flowing with milk and honey." (AMP)**

The Hebrew word for delight is ***chaphets (Khaw-fates)*** which means to incline, to bend, pleased, desire, favor.

God's desire was to take the Israelites into the Promised Land that was filled with milk and honey. He knew there were giants in the land but He had planned a way of escape. He had favor and blessings waiting for them, however, they needed to trust and obey for there was no other way to live in this Promise Land.

Let's face it as long as the enemy can keep our focus on what we did, what others did to us and giant situations that surround us . . . we won't focus on what Jesus has already done by dying on the cross to save us from our sin! As long as we keep our focus on the sin we will not be able to focus on Jesus who became all of our sin.

> **I John 3: 5 says, "You know that He appeared in visible form *and* became Man to take away (upon Himsel) sins, and in Him there is no sin (essentially and forever)." (AMP)**

Just as Mommy delights in me even when I'm not following all of her commands, she knows that eventually I will. So . . . . she waits patiently for me with a delicious treat in her hands. Your Daddy God delights in you and is waiting patiently for you to follow His commands! He is here to pick you up on His shoulders today so you can delight in each other! Will you come?

Where is Your Treasure?

Every morning my daddy gives me biscuits and some treats. I love to put them into my mouth and run into the living room and lay each one down. During the day, I proudly display them in my mouth but continue to save some of them. Sometimes Mommy comes along and scoops them up. Believe me . . . I watch where she places them. After all, they are my treasures!

Luke 12:34 says, "Where your treasure is there will your heart be also." (NIV)

Treasures are riches accumulated or possessed or one who is regarded as valuable, precious or rare. Who or what do you treasure? Mommy says that we are to love God with all of our heart, mind and soul. Now that seems really hard to understand, doesn't it? I know that God loves me and Mommy and Daddy with a love that never ends. Wow! That's a **Great Love**! After all, He sent His son, Jesus to die on the cross for all of us. He died so we could live with Him on earth and in heaven. But . . . how do we live with Him on earth? Mommy said when she was going through a dark trial in her life, she began to really know God . . . not just know about Him! She said that one day the Holy Spirit spoke this to her, "My people would love me if they knew me!" She said she could feel the sadness in His heart for the people that didn't know Him. Mommy says that she really treasures her relationship with God. Every day she comes to talk to Him . . . . then she says He talks to her! Sometimes I crawl up beside Mommy and try to listen to God too! But . . . . I never hear Him like she does. She says that's because He speaks in a very small voice in our spirit. I think she means in our insides. Mommy says when you go through trials in your life you either run to God or run away from Him. Oh! I just got this thought that makes me shudder! What if I would have run away when I was sick so my mommy and daddy couldn't find me? There would have been no one to help me and I believe that I would have died.

Are you going through a hard trial in your life today? If so, are you running to God or running away from Him? Or maybe you are so discouraged that you feel stuck where you are. Believe me . . . I remember those days when I was too sick to even kiss Daddy and Mommy or crawl up in their lap. Oh! I wanted to but I just couldn't seem to muster up the energy. I kept thinking of how I was going to die. But . . . my daddy and mommy kept asking Jesus to heal me. Yessiree! Jesus gave me the best Daddy and Mommy in the whole world!

Colossians 3:2 says, "Set your mind on things above, not on things on the earth." (NIV)

Where are your thoughts right now? Are you thinking about how bad things are or how good your Daddy God is? One day Mommy was feeling low but didn't know why. So . . . she asked God what was wrong. He told her that she was disappointed and she needed to tell Him about it. She said, "Lord, I give you these disappointments!" He said, "I want you to give them to me in detail!" Well, Mommy said that a whole bunch of words started coming out of her mouth concerning what was disappointing her. She hadn't even realized she had been carrying these disappointments in her heart. After saying these words she felt so much better!

Guess what! You have the best Daddy God in the whole wide world! Are you disappointed with love from others? No one can love you like Jesus! After all, His arms were stretched out on the cross to show how much He loves you. His arms are reaching out to help you now. Won't you reach back and receive His love for you today? Hmmm! What would happen if you make a list of your disappointments and give them to Jesus today? I bet you'll feel so much better too! Better yet . . . let's give them to Jesus together!

Jesus, I have so many disappointments that I don't know where to begin. So I'm asking you to reveal what is inside of me so I can give them to you.

Now talk to Jesus about these disappointments and you will experience His freedom today!

Putin on a Tude!

Did you ever have days where you feel like nothing suits you? It seems like no one is listening to what you want and you just aren't getting your way?

Well, I guess this is confession time. Actually did you know that confession is good for the soul? Sometimes my daddy makes me do things I don't want to . . . like bringing home a new sweater that's called a doggie blanket! Of all things! First of all, I don't see myself as a doggie since I'm more sophisticated than that. Did anybody ever misunderstand you? Well, I get that all the time! I am a very good communicator yet people don't always understand what I want!

Well, back to this so called doggie blanket. First of all, you never wear a blanket you just cover with it. I looked up the definition of blanket. It is a bed covering or an area that covers something completely. Now, I ask you for your opinion. Do you really think I can wear a blanket? How dumb do they think I am? This thing you have to wear like a sweater. C'mon do you think I can be completely covered? How could I ever walk or take care of my necessities? So . . . why don't they call it a sweater? I'll tell you why! They want to sell a new idea that you can tell everybody about. After all, new things are all the rage! Well, Daddy was trying to get me to wear it. Guess what! No instructions came with the box! Boy! Doesn't that just upset you when you buy something new without instructions?

When there are no instructions, it takes so much longer to figure it out! Daddy kept trying all different ways and believe me

I was getting mighty impatient. Mommy took one look at me and saw my tude! Now, mind you I didn't bite or growl or show my teeth! I wouldn't think of doing that! But . . . . I was getting mighty impatient and it showed on my face!

Do you ever get impatient? Mommy says that patience is the key that unlocks the door to God's heart! I don't quite understand that! But . . . I guess that means that God is pleased when we wait on Him! Well, to be honest, I don't like waiting! I want to play when I want to play and eat when I want to eat! My daddy had been away and I wanted him to play with my toys and chase me. I didn't want to wait to have to put a dumb old doggie blanket on that was named wrong. But . . . Daddy kept insisting that I hold still and wait till he placed it on me. Well, I made up my mind that I would hold still for Daddy but I wasn't going to enjoy this so I put my disgusted face on. But . . . you can't fool my daddy! He knew that I was feeling impatient and very irritated even though I didn't say any words!

Do you ever put a disgusted face on? Well, your Daddy God knows your heart even if you don't say it. Sometimes we act like a little goody two shoes but underneath that phi sod there is a strong irritation. Actually, I have to admit this since it's confession time! I started out being irritated by that dumb doggie blanket but ended up being irritated with my daddy for making me wait!

Jeremiah 17: 9 in The Message says, "The heart is hopelessly dark and deceitful, a puzzle that no one can figure out. But I, GOD, search the heart and examine the mind. I get to the heart of the human. I get to the root of things. I treat them as they really are, not as they pretend to be."

Now, the question is . . . are you irritated with your Daddy God? Believe me I know how hard it is to admit that because I love my daddy so much. But . . . just like I don't fool my daddy . . . you aren't fooling yours! And . . . you will feel so much better when you admit it! So . . . talk to your Daddy God today. Did you know that unconfessed sin blocks us from receiving God's love for us? How about we confess this together?

> **Lord, please forgive me for being upset and irritated with You. I really have a hard time in waiting for the answers to my prayers so I need Your help. I ask you to look in my heart and show me what displeases You. I give You my plans and ask you to place Your plan for my life on my heart in Jesus' Name. Amen.**

See! I told you confession is good for the soul! Don't you feel so much better? I know I do!

Step under God's Shower

Have you ever been outside while it was raining? There are days that I have to be out in the yard to take care of business. Well, it's not too much fun coming in with muddy paws and tracking mud the whole way up the steps! Especially, when Mommy sees the mud and says, "Okay, Danny, it's time to get a **bath**!"

Oh! Don't you just hate that terrible word . . . . **bath**? I don't know about you but I put my head and tail down to the floor and don't budge while Mommy tries to coax me to go with Daddy. Believe me . . . I know what it means to get a **bath**! Actually, I would rather be dirty than go through a cleansing process which I view as very grueling! No . . . I didn't say growling. But believe me I sure do feel like growling since I know that this will be extremely exhausting! Especially, since I will try to jump out of the tub while Daddy gives me that terrible word . . . **bath**! Well, Mommy says that God wants us to have a **bath** too! No . . . I'm not talking about physical hygiene for just your physical health. I'm talking about emotional cleanliness for your physical, emotional and spiritual health!

Mommy says that she doesn't like getting her hair wet under the shower. Hmm! I just realized that I'm a lot like my mommy. Well, one day she had this vision during worship in her church. She saw herself under a shower with her head back so as not to get her hair wet. The Holy Spirit spoke in her heart that He wanted to cleanse all of her . . . not just certain areas. He encouraged Mommy to step under His shower! Mommy says that we are all muddied with fear, worry, unforgiveness, selfishness, pride, jealousy and so forth!

Mommy says that God is calling all of His children to step under His shower.

> **Psalm 139:23-24 says, "Search me, O God, and know my heart; test me and know my anxious thoughts and see if there is any offensive ways in me and lead me in the way everlasting." (NIV)**

Well, Mommy and Daddy saw all the mud that was on me since I left a trail. Sometimes we all leave trails for other people to clean up instead of asking God to clean us up! Mommy says the Hebrew meaning for search is to penetrate or examine intimately. Wow! I think that means when we get really close to God, He begins to show us truth about ourselves that can sometimes be very painful.

Think about the friends with whom you have a close relationship. In the beginning you didn't know each other but eventually as you spent time together, you developed a close relationship with one another. With some friends we become so close that we begin to let our hair down and get real with each other. In that relationship a trust begins to form which sometimes lead to painful truths because we love them.

But . . . . you need to understand when God shows us our mud we need to allow Him to clean us up! When I get **a bath** my daddy has to start at my back end, since I am very fearful of putting my head under the water first. In other words, Daddy eases me into the process. Guess what! You can rest assured that your Daddy God knows where to begin cleaning you up! He will ease you into the process when you are ready to experience His freedom and not view it as a grueling process. So . . . do you have an intimate relationship with the Lord? If so, are you allowing Him to penetrate your heart and reveal His truth?

Believe me . . . I don't like the cleaning process any more than you do. But . . . . afterwards, I really feel free. I run and jump like a little puppy all around the house. Mommy laughs when she sees how free I am. And of course, I smell so . . . . good!

Well, are you ready to smell like the fragrance of Jesus? Let's pray this together.

Jesus, I give you permission to examine my heart and mind. I want you to remove all the mud in me. Thank you for revealing fear, anger, unforgiveness, selfishness, worry, jealousy and those anxious thoughts. Lead me on your path and not my own in Jesus' Name. Amen.

Now . . . . wait for the Holy Spirit to reveal those areas of weaknesses and give them to Him so that He can begin the cleansing process! You'll be glad you did!

Drowning in Despair

Have you ever felt like you are drowning in despair? Well, I certainly have when I was so ill. I was so sick that I thought I was going to die and would never see Daddy and Mommy again. But . . . let me tell you of another time. One day I was sitting on top of our couch looking out the window for my daddy to come home. You see, he had gone away and didn't take me. Well, I was very disappointed about this. The longer I sat on the cushions, the deeper they began to sink in. Mommy tried to fluff the cushions to lift me higher but it was impossible since they were losing their shape.

Well, I felt like I was beginning to get bent out of shape like those cushions. I was so upset that my daddy wasn't home. Every car that went by I followed by turning my head and watching through the window. Actually, I always feel like that until Mommy says, "Danny, Daddy won't be gone long!" That really helps to ease my fears.

Mommy was reminded of a song called, "Love lifted me!" The first part is "I was sinking deep in sin far from the peaceful shore, very deeply stained within sinking to rise no more. But the Master of the sea heard my despairing cry from the waters' lifted me now safe am I." Do you feel like you can barely keep your head above water? Is there so much happening in your life that has caused you to despair?

II Corinthians 4:7-9 says, "But we have this treasure in jars of clay to show that this all surpassing power is

**from God and not from us. We are hard pressed on every
side, but not crushed; perplexed, but not in despair;
persecuted, but not abandoned; struck down, but not
destroyed." (NIV)**

So . . . what is the treasure? The Greek meaning of treasure is
deposit, wealth. In other words, when you asked Jesus into your
heart, you received His deposit of great wealth. No wealth on
earth can compare with the wealth you have inside to conquer the
enemy's lies. Believe me . . . your treasure within is much greater
than any treasures you have on earth. For example, my treats and
biscuits only last for a certain amount of time and then I have to
ask Daddy for more of them. I have a very favorite biscuit that has
chicken in it. Oh! Boy! I really love chicken! Daddy gives me one
a day. However, I have experienced days when the bag was empty
and I had to wait for Daddy to buy more for me.

Great News! You don't have to wait for your treasure. The Holy
Spirit within you is your great wealth! He is never empty! In II
Corinthians 7:5, the Apostle Paul gives us more detail on what
troubled on every side means, He says, **"Outside was afflictions
and inside was fears!"**

Now, I don't mind telling you that I was fearful of my daddy
not coming back for a long time or not at all. Remember in my
testimony I told you that I had been abandoned two times. Yes, I
had other people around me in the SPCA but I no longer had the
people that I thought loved me. Abandonment is a really hard thing
to get over. Mommy says that since I was rejected I now project
that rejection onto thinking that my daddy and mommy will reject
me too. I guess that means that I expect them to reject me since I'm
always thinking they will leave me. Sometimes I almost panic when
I see them getting ready to go away. I follow them around and put
my saddest face on so they will take pity on me. Sometimes I even
convince them to say yes when they weren't planning on taking me
along.

Mommy says that when we accept Jesus into our heart, we
are now part of His family. I guess that's just like me since I am

now a part of Daddy and Mommy's family too. She says that God adopted us into His family and has a great adventure ahead for us!

> **Romans 8:15 (The Message) says, "This resurrection life you received from God is not a timid, grave-tending life. It's adventurously expectant, greeting God with a childlike 'What's next, Papa?' God's Spirit touches our spirits and confirms who we really are. We know who he is, and we know who we are: Father and children. And we know we are going to get what's coming to us—an unbelievable inheritance! We go through exactly what Christ goes through. If we go through the hard times with him, then we're certainly going to go through the good times with him!"**

Wow! When you realize God's acceptance for you as His child . . . rejection won't get through the front door of your mind. Maybe some of you have been abandoned or rejected by other people. Think of this! Your Daddy God loves and accepts you just the way you are and will never leave or forsake you! Okay, it's time to be honest! Are you sinking in an ocean filled with fear that has carried you into despair? If so, can we pray this together?

> **Jesus, I have been sinking in an ocean filled with despair. I give you this fear of abandonment and rejection. I need your love to lift me into your peace, love and forgiveness and ask you to reveal any hidden fears within my heart. Thank You for showing me who You are and who I am in You! You are my Daddy God and I am Your child! Thank You for Your unbelievable inheritance and for lifting me up out of the despair. I wait with great expectation for You to show Yourself strong in Jesus' Name. Amen.**

Now . . . doesn't that make you feel better?

What are Your Temptations?

Chocolate cream eggs are one of Mommy's favorite. As she was checking out of a store one day, they were sitting in front of her calling out her name! She yielded to the temptation and bought only one and placed it in her purse with full intentions of devouring this egg all by herself!

One day I had been looking all through the house to find Mommy. I don't like her being out of my sight for too long so I thought I'd better check up on her. Then I smelled something sweet and heard wrappers being opened. I found Mommy sitting on the floor enjoying a delicious coconut cream egg. So . . . . I began to beg her to give me a bite. Mommy gave me a taste of the coconut that tasted so . . . . good! Boy! It was so yummy! But . . . she wrapped up the rest of it and kept it in her purse.

A couple of days later Mommy had to give Daddy something out of her purse. She was in a hurry so she left her opened purse on the bed. I remembered that delicious coconut and thought this was my chance to help myself! Well, the paper was still on it so I decided that I would bring that temptation to Mommy. Now you need to understand . . . this was a very strong temptation for me. I wanted to open up the paper and eat all of it. I love the smell of chocolate but Mommy had told me before that chocolate isn't good for me and will make me very sick! Frankly, I wasn't into being sick and knew that Mommy would give me the coconut without the chocolate! Now the next move was to strategically place this egg in my mouth so as not to have any bite marks or any saliva on this egg. You also need to know that this coconut egg was so small that I could have definitely managed to remove all of the paper from it.

Mommy was sitting in a chair in the living room. I walked up to her and gently nudged against her legs. Immediately she looked down at me. Now if you can picture this! I had this coconut cream egg that had been wrapped in saran wrap just barely holding it in my mouth. Immediately Mommy placed her hand under my mouth and said, "Danny, drop it!" Of course, I did! Mommy was so proud of me. I willingly gave this temptation over and didn't put up a fight! Mommy could barely keep from laughing since I guess I looked pretty silly! But the best part of all was that she gave me more coconut!

Mommy says we have lots of temptations daily. But . . . we have to make a choice to give our temptations over to God. I am reminded about a story in the Bible on Adam and Eve. From the very beginning, they had the goodness of the Lord. Can you imagine walking and talking with God in a beautiful garden every day without a care in the world? My daddy takes me for a walk every day and I really enjoy being with him. I have a certain time of the day that I begin to nudge my daddy to take me for a walk. If Daddy doesn't pay attention to me right away, I make sure he does by jumping on him and kissing his ears.

If I try to get too far ahead of Daddy while we are walking he pulls me back. Or if I am tempted to wander off in another direction other than where Daddy wants to take me . . . again he pulls me back.

God placed a tree of restriction in front of Adam and Eve with the consequences of death if they would eat of its fruit. However, the serpent that was more crafty and subtle than any creature said to Eve, **"You shall not surely die. God knows that in the day you eat of it your eyes will be opened and you will be like God, knowing the difference between good and evil and blessing and calamity!" (Genesis 3:4-5 NIV)**

"And when the woman saw that the tree was good (suitable and pleasant) for food and that it was delightful to look at, and a tree to be desired in order to make one wise, she took of

its fruit and ate; and she gave some also to her husband, and he ate." (Genesis 3:6 AMP) Did you catch how the fruit on the tree was pleasing to her senses? It seemed to be calling her name just like the coconut cream egg called Mommy and me. It was good, delightful and pleasant. But . . . isn't that how sin is in the beginning? So . . . what was the problem? Satan was putting doubts in her mind by saying, "Did God really say that? C'mon you can eat just a little bit!" Isn't that what we hear in our mind when we are tempted to sin? Satan whispers doubt and unbelief and tries to sweep the consequences away from the disobedience which causes us to bite into the temptation. Yet God calls us to obedience since He knows the consequences will not be swept away!

Eve's focus was no longer on loving God and obeying Him . . . . but on the temptation of eating the fruit. Hmmm! I wonder what would have happened if Eve would have brought her temptation to God like I did to Mommy. I bet it would have changed the whole wide world. When I brought that coconut cream egg to Mommy I didn't get sick and she rewarded me with more coconut! If Eve would have looked for God and brought the fruit to Him, her life would have been blessed and she and her family wouldn't have gotten sick.

Well, now that I've told you my temptation . . . what is yours? Notice . . . I had to make a choice not to unwrap the egg knowing that it would taste so good but in the end I would end up really sick.

When the enemy comes in like a flood the spirit of the Lord will rise up against it. Your spirit needs to say no to sin and yes to God! No matter what temptation you are facing, God is here right now to help you! Just as Mommy placed her hand at my mouth for me to drop the egg in her hand, God is reaching out His hand for you to drop the temptation in the palm of His hand! **I Corinthians 10:13 says, "When you are tempted, He will show you a way out so that you will not give into it. No temptation has overtaken you except such as is common to man; but God is faithful who will not allow you to be tempted beyond what** you are able but with the temptation will also make the way of escape that you may be able to bear it!"

> II Peter 2:9 says, "Now if (all these things are true, then be sure) the Lord knows how to rescue the godly out of temptations *and* trials, and how to keep the ungodly under chastisement until the day of judgment *and* doom." (AMP)

Are you ready to drop it? If so, let's pray together!

> Jesus you promised that you won't allow me to be overtaken by temptations. I give you (name your temptations) and ask that you would rescue me from them. I know that you are a faithful God and will make a way of escape that I will be able to bear it. I will wait with great expectation for you to show yourself strong in my life in Jesus' Name. Amen.

The next time a temptation comes along remember this prayer that you and I prayed. God has a great way of escape for you!

Who has the Last Word?

Mommy was down on the floor playing with me. She noticed that one of my toys had a hole and the stuffing was falling out. She tried to take the toy out of my mouth while I playfully growled at her. She began to imitate my growl but I always had the last growl. After all, I wasn't going to let Mommy have my toy until I was ready to give it up! Mommy said, "Danny, you just want to have the last word!"

Mommy knew that it wasn't good for me to swallow the stuffing but I didn't want to let go. I wasn't done playing with my toy and was enjoying every minute of running from Mommy. She didn't want me to swallow any stuffing from that toy since she knew it could harm me. **But** . . . I wasn't willing to let go.

So . . . let's talk about the word. **BUT**! Now we know that **but** is a conjunction used to connect words, phrases or clauses. I realized that God speaks His word to us and we have a choice to obey or to **but** His word!

My mommy was trying to take my toy that could have harmed me if I swallowed the stuffing. **But** . . . I was insisting on my own way when I held onto my toy! I even had to have the last growl! God's word says to forgive and we say, "**But** God, didn't you see how they treated me?" His word says to love your neighbor as yourself and we say, "**But** God, they aren't showing me any love?" And what about . . . God will never leave or forsake us? We say, "**But** God, I don't feel your presence anymore!" What about be angry and sin not! We say, "**But** God, they deserve it!" God has the best plan for our life and we say, "**But** God, don't you know that I have great plans already?"

Did you ever hear the saying that he is mule headed? I believe that sometimes God sees that display in us. Picture yourself coming behind a mule and being kicked since he has no intention of doing what you want. Oh! My goodness! I wouldn't think of going behind a mule! Do you really think that God wants too?

Mommy said that one morning during worship she was telling God how much she loved Him. She asked Him how she could show more love to Him. He said, "Love the unlovely!" Now . . . it was her choice to choose to love and receive God's blessing or choose her way of disobedience and **BUT** the God she loved!

Many things that happen in this life look impossible to solve . . . **BUT** GOD! Aha! I guess this is when God has the last word! Actually, that is a divine conjunction when we no longer make demands but see what God can do when we choose His way! Mommy can't love the unlovely by her own love. **But** . . . she can love others with God's love that is in her insides! **"Every Word of God is tried and purified. He is a shield to those who trust and take refuge in Him!" (Proverbs 30:5 AMP)**

Word is taken from the Hebrew which means commandment. God doesn't give His suggestions . . . He commands the best to free us from our sins.

So . . . is your **BUT** a divine or demand conjunction? If you are saying, **"But** God" and demanding your own way . . . please pray this prayer with me.

> **Jesus . . . I am sorry for demanding my own way and not listening to Your ways! I ask You to forgive me for being selfish. I no longer want to be mule headed but choose to listen to Your Words for my life. I know that your plan is the best! I take refuge in You and thank You for being my shield in Jesus' Name. Amen!**

Now . . . if you said this prayer, begin to thank God for His blessings!

But..I want to go bye byes!

Are you following
Jesus' Example?

Mommy was going through a tough time of rejection from being wounded by someone. She says that her flesh wanted to let other people know what had happened. However, she knew that God would not be pleased with her words.

> **"You have proved my heart You have visited *me* in the night; You have tried me and find nothing [no evil purpose in me]; I have purposed that my mouth shall not transgress." (Psalm 17:3 AMP)**

Well, I guess that means that God doesn't want you to say things that will hurt other people. That reminds me of the time another precious lady in the ministry team brought her new little puppy, Hunter. This little guy couldn't contain his excitement and immediately started chasing me. Now remember, I am not very good with dogs that are aggressive even if they are a puppy. At one point, even though I knew Mommy wouldn't be happy with me, I growled at Hunter and began chasing him. Mommy said, "Danny, you didn't like Hunter chasing you. Now don't chase him.

> **Matthew 7:12 says, "So then whatever you desire that others would do to and for you so do also to and for them for this is (sums up) the law and the prophets." (AMP)**

Many of you know this scripture as the "Golden Rule"! Yet, sometimes we change the words to suit ourselves. Notice . . . . it doesn't say, "Do unto others before they get you or do unto others as they do to you." Well, I'm sorry to say that I was chasing and growling at Hunter since he was doing the same to me. However, Hunter's motive was playful and mine was revengeful! But, what if his motive was not playful? Would I still have the right to hurt him back?

Leviticus 19:18 says, "You shall not take revenge or bear any grudge against the sons of your people, but you shall love your neighbor as yourself. I am the Lord." (AMP)

Whoa! That is a tall order, isn't it? Mommy says we have to choose to forgive and not let our emotions rule us. I guess she means that it's our choice to forgive or hurt other people with our words. Sometimes people don't mean to hurt us but it's their insensitivity that causes us pain. Mommy says that we need to think about how we want others to treat us. She says when she makes mistakes she needs mercy from God and other people. There are times when she feels worn out and needs words of encouragement or hugs and smiles from others. Believe me I really try to encourage Mommy when she is feeling discouraged and cries. I cuddle up beside her and kiss her tears! Mommy begins to laugh and that helps to make me feel better too! Mommy says when she talks to Jesus and asks Him to use her as His vessel of mercy, encouragement, love, peace and forgiveness, He places people in her path that amaze her. She says that every one of us have times that we are insensitive to other people's needs.

In John 13:15 after Jesus washed His disciple's feet; He tells them that He is their example. He showed them that He was a servant to all of them and they are to follow His example in being a servant to others.

Micah 6:8 says, "And what does the Lord require of you but to do justly, love mercy and walk humbly with your God." (NIV)

Notice . . . this is a requirement that you can do when you walk humbly with your God. It doesn't say, "You must do this alone". Believe me I need a lot of help in being nice to some dogs since they can rub me the wrong way.

Proverbs 27:17 says, "Iron sharpens iron; so a man sharpens the countenance of his friend (to show rage or worthy purpose). (AMP)

Oh! Boy! That doesn't feel so good, does it? But . . . you can't follow someone's example if you don't know them. So the question is . . . Do you know Jesus? If you know Him, are you following His example in being a servant to others no matter what? Or, are you doing to others as they do to you?

Will you pray this with me?

Jesus . . . Your Word says that I am to do unto others as I would like them to do to me. Forgive me for giving only what I receive from others and not giving when I don't receive. Thank you for giving me your strength, courage and ability to forgive and have mercy on others as you have given me mercy and forgiveness. Use me as your vessel by placing someone in my path that needs a smile, hug or word of encouragement today in Jesus' Name. Amen.

Boy! I'm making the choice to be nice to other dogs and even cats. Well, maybe some! How about you? What choices are you making?

What's been happening?

I'm sure that many of you are wondering how I am doing now? I can hardly believe that it has been over one year since my operation. We are so thankful to God and the veterinarians that He used to help save my life. I have even more energy now than I did five years ago. I even eat more which amazes Mommy and Daddy.

Well, it sure has been great to teach you these lessons. Do you know that God has lessons to teach you every day? Sometimes we just have to listen. Did you know that you can learn more by listening than talking! At least that's what my daddy always says. Sometimes we have happy endings but sometimes they are sad. Remember when I told you my grandpa was sick in his kidneys? Well, he went home to be with Jesus in May 2012. My daddy was really sad but he knew that his daddy went to heaven and that helped to ease his pain and sorrow. Life is so hard to understand, isn't it? Yet when we keep walking and talking with Jesus daily, He gives us peace in the midst of storms in our lives. By the way, I don't have glaucoma in my eyes but I do have cataracts on both of them. About two months ago Mommy had another dream. This time Mommy was standing at a swimming pool. She was holding me in her arms. Suddenly I jumped out of her arms and into the swimming pool. Mommy said that she noticed when I went down to the bottom of the pool, my eyes were opened and I could see clearly! Afterwards, I swam to the top and went down to the bottom of the pool again. Mommy saw my eyes opened and no cataracts. I was so excited when Mommy told me about this dream. We believe that God is going to heal my eyes completely! After all, if God decrees it . . . it will happen! I'm so thankful that I have a Mommy and Daddy that love Jesus. It sure makes my life easier. I know they pray for a lot of people and have compassion for them. Mommy's daddy went home to be with Jesus ten years ago and her baby brother joined him two years later. By the way, Mommy reminded me to inform you that all of these events that I have relayed to you in my testimony and the lessons are spot on!

Well, Jesus taught Mommy a lot of lessons in those valleys. Actually, Mommy says if we stay close to God He will teach us lessons in the valleys that we could never learn on the mountaintops! Maybe you are in a valley in your life right now. Jesus wants you to know that He is right beside you and will see you through this trial in your life. He has a great plan for you! Keep holding His hand and don't let go!

About the Author

Jenny Hagemeyer was born in Altoona, Pa. At the age of six she ran to the altar out of fear of going to hell and accepted the Lord into her heart at a CMA church. Her parents later moved to Lancaster County, Pa where she grew up and graduated from high school. Her desire was to be a missionary and attend a Bible school but unforeseen circumstances took place and didn't allow that to happen. She met a young man after graduation and married at the age of eighteen years old. Throughout those years Jenny taught Sunday school, held Bible studies in her home, good news clubs for children and counseled at church camps. However, in those years, she only knew God as a Bible God.

In 1982 Jenny received the Baptism of the Holy Spirit in an Aglow meeting that her friend had taken her too. As an adult she would still cower in fear while praying and telling God that she was a bad girl. One day as she was praying she heard the Holy Spirit say, "What kind of a God do you think I am?" In 1983 a bombshell was dropped on her that would change the rest of her life. Her son was diagnosed with severe scoliosis, her husband of fifteen years left on her daughter's twelfth birthday, their dog was put to sleep and her uncle died suddenly whom she loved. This began her journey to a more intimate relationship with the Lord. One night, during the separation, the Lord spoke to her in an audible voice. He told her that He was going to use her to heal His people. He said, "You must be able to hear my voice!" Jenny had no idea how God could use her while she was so distraught in her emotions that there was no way she could help herself let alone other people!

In 1987 Jenny married Fred from Mifflin County, Pa whom she met in a Christian singles group in Lancaster County. Afterwards she felt a strong calling from the Lord to be used in ministry and began to seek the Lord for His direction and guidance.

In 1998 she started a women's weight loss group in her home. The Lord gave her a vision of a heart that looked like a puzzle with many pieces. Beside the heart was a bag of presents. God showed Jenny when she gave those pieces, such as anger, unforgiveness, selfishness, pride, fear, jealousies and so forth over to Him the blessings would come such as peace, love, joy, patience, goodness, meekness, kindness, gentleness and self control. God showed Jenny that her heart was clogged like a drain gets clogged in a sink and she needed His Drano of love to penetrate those darkened areas in her heart. The women's group consisted of women of different denominations and backgrounds. As Jenny and the other women talked with one another, they realized they all had low self esteem and didn't like themselves! As God began to reveal those areas in Jenny, she began to teach those lessons weekly to the other women. God began a healing process in Jenny's past that has enabled her to teach it out to many others. As she yielded to the Holy Spirit He placed a message in her heart. He told her, "It's time to heal the church to heal the world!"

Jenny and the other women began to pray Psalm 26:2 daily that says, **"Test me, O Lord and try me, examine my heart and mind for your love is ever before me and I walk continually in your truth."** God began to reveal areas in their heart that needed healed. They learned to lay them at the feet of Jesus and ask Him to change them! As they opened the door to the closet of their heart that contained fear, unforgiveness, selfishness, pride and so forth God began construction in all of them.

Jenny is the author of the books, "Touch Me" and Touch Me Guide to Healing" written under the inspiration of the Holy Spirit that shares her journey to a more intimate relationship with the Lord that brought healing to her heart and mind. It is a life giving study that brings encouragement in which Jenny shares openly the locked emotions that became imprisoned in her heart, negative thoughts that she entertained and hurtful words that were spoken about her and to her. Jenny teaches the "Touch Me" study in churches and prisons. She shares her testimony of how God led her to put God's WORD into action in not only being a hearer of the WORD but a doer! Ultimately, God led her into a teaching of what God's desire of an abundant life represents.

She is a speaker called by God to take His message of love out to the highways and byways. Promise Land Ministries is available for retreats, renewals, workshops, special programs and other events. Every ministry event is tailored by the Holy Spirit to meet the emotional, physical and spiritual needs of the people. For more information on the ministry see the blog at promiselandministries. wordpress.com.

To contact Jenny write:
Jenny Hagemeyer
76 Shawnee Drive
Belleville, Pa 17004

Please include a testimony of how "Lessons from Danny" has touched your heart. This book will also be available on an audio book in the iUniverse bookstore!